Signs, Wonders, and Miracles

History of the Saints

Signs, Wonders, and Miracles

Extraordinary Stories from Early Latter-day Saints

EDITED BY
GLENN RAWSON & DENNIS LYMAN

Covenant Communications, Inc.

Cover images:
Arrival of Brigham Young © Valoy Eaton—www.foundationarts.com
Patience Loader © Julie Roger— www.julierogersart.com
Harshness of Winter © L Curley Christensen— www.lindacurley.com
Day of God's Power © Liz Lemon Swindle—www.foundationarts.com

Published by Covenant Communications, Inc.
American Fork, Utah

Printed in the United States of America
First Printing: October 2015

21 20 19 18 17 16 15 10 9 8 7 6 5 4 3 2 1

ISBN 978-1-68047-668-2

The Lord promised us that "signs shall follow them that believe" (Mark 16:17), and then He explained what some of those signs would be—casting out devils, speaking in new tongues, and healings, to mention just a few. It is a truth that wherever the Lord's people are found, there will be signs, wonders, and miracles among them.

This book is an anthology—a collection of stories with a single theme—that shows that the Lord worked mighty miracles among the first generation of Latter-day Saints. Some of these stories are about people with whom we are all familiar, but a significant number are about faithful pioneers known only to their descendants. In some instances, the stories demonstrate the merciful intervention of heaven; in other cases, the angels were mortals and courage and compassion were the miracles.

For help in telling these stories, the editors have turned to some of the foremost scholars in Church Education—those who are, for the most part, trained as historians and researchers. By so doing, not only do we get those stories not often heard, but the stories are good history.

The intent of this work is to inspire and edify. The pioneers were ordinary people who accomplished extraordinary things by the Lord's grace. It is our hope that by studying their lives we will be strengthened to do likewise.

Table of Contents

"A Branch of My Calling"

By Glenn Rawson

Writer, producer, and host of the
Joseph Smith Papers and History of the Saints television series

Very great doors turn on small hinges, meaning that "by small and simple things are great things brought to pass" (Alma 37:6). Never was this truer than in this instance.

No sooner was the Book of Mormon off Grandin's press in Palmyra than Joseph was reassigned. The project is little known and even less understood, even by Joseph's own people. Yet it was so critical a work that he devoted much of his time to it for more than two years. The endeavor was launched as a commandment from the Almighty Himself and shepherded by Him to its completion. Joseph would later call this monumental work a "branch of [his] calling."

It was known and prophesied millennia before that Joseph would do this work. Moses himself looked forward to it. It was an integral component of the Restoration. So much of Joseph's doctrine—so many of the great revelations of the Restoration—came because of this effort.

The contribution of this work to the corpus of Latter-day Saint theology is incalculable. Its contribution to the personal education and edification of Joseph Smith himself was vast.

Today many of us hold it in our hands, pack it off to Church, and seldom appreciate what we have. What is it? The Joseph Smith Translation of the Bible.

As to what the Joseph Smith Translation is and its attendant power, the Lord told Joseph at the outset, "The scriptures shall be given even as they are in mine own bosom to the salvation of mine own elect" (D&C 35:20).

How did it come to be? A scribe sat waiting with paper, pen, and ink. Joseph sat down with the large family Bible he had purchased from E. B. Grandin and began to read under the influence of the Holy Ghost. As he read without the aid of seer stones or the Urim and Thummim, his mind was opened, inspired, and enlightened. As he passed through reading the text, he dictated changes. Sometimes there were no changes; sometimes the changes were as minor as correcting punctuation, spelling, or grammar. Other times there were small deletions. But most impressively, sometimes whole chapters detailing intricate narratives of doctrine and history— such as the writings about Enoch or Joseph of Egypt—were revealed to Joseph.

From the fountain of his expanded mind, Joseph would dictate these new passages to his scribe, word for word, at a pace slow enough to be written down longhand—and he did it without ever losing his train of thought, having to start over, or having to gather his creativity. Just the process, as described by witnesses, is miraculous considering the material revealed, but the miracle becomes utterly astonishing when the work is carefully studied and pondered. How could a twenty-seven-year-old uneducated farmer from the frontier have produced such a work? It is inconceivable—making the Joseph Smith Translation another tangible testament with the Book of Mormon that Joseph Smith was a prophet of God.

Many have opined that he never finished it or that its text was adulterated after he died, but both ideas are false. Perhaps its greatest contribution is its witness of the Savior. The Joseph Smith Translation reveals a greater Christ—more noble, and even more divine, making the Joseph Smith Translation another testament of Christ and the most correct of any Bible on earth.

Source

http://josephsmithpapers.org/searchNew?query=Branch%20of%20my%20Calling&sort=relevance&page=1&perpage=10&startdate=&enddate=&transcripts=false&issuggestion=false&types=documents-papers|documents-papers-histories|related-materials|biographical-directory|geographical-directory|glossary.

"A Fighter and a Gentleman"

By Julie Parkin
English teacher

The Lord said to Joshua, "Be strong and of a good courage; be not afraid" (Joshua 1:9). Such righteous strength and courage is so vitally needed now and will change the world. And so it did for John Parkin on a busy street in Loscoe, Derbyshire, in 1849.

As he walked down a street in his native England, John came upon a large, noisy crowd; at the center was an English Mormon missionary, Elder Aaron Nelson. As the missionary tried to preach to those assembled, he was repeatedly interrupted by three well-known ministers whose comments were generally supported as the crowd jeered and laughed.

John wasn't interested in Mormonism, but after observing long enough to see that the man was being mercilessly heckled, he called in a strong voice, "I know nothing about the doctrines of this man, but I believe in free speech and fair play. If you ministers want to dispute the elder's religion, you may, but you must wait until he finishes his speech."

John's admonishment quieted the crowd momentarily, but soon the jeers and shouts resumed, led by the ministers. John shook his fist at the preachers and yelled, "I don't know this man, but he looks and talks decently, and he has got to have a hearing, [even] if I have to smash the men that interrupt him."

While John was not a fighter by profession, he was skilled at it and was in possession of a strong body and considerable self-confidence.

When one of the ministers continued his badgering, John grabbed him by the collar and threatened him again. The man's burly son rushed forward and took a swing at John, who nimbly sidestepped the punch and struck one of his own with such force that his attacker dropped like a stone.

"Come on, now, all of you, one at a time, and I'll whip the entire crowd!" John shouted. Luckily for all, it began to rain, and the crowd quickly dispersed.

When John learned that Elder Nelson lived some miles away and had no local shelter, John invited the missionary to his home to wait out the storm. By evening, it became apparent no one would be able to travel that night. When the elder joined the family for dinner, they politely listened to his religious beliefs.

Later that night, asking permission to offer a prayer before retiring, the missionary was told the family was not religious; nonetheless, permission was granted. In his prayer, Elder Nelson thanked God for the one man in Loscoe who would accept the truth.

In their chamber that night, John discussed with his wife the elder's odd words: one man who would accept the truth—what did that mean? In the morning, John asked the elder to explain his statement, and he answered, "You are the man."

Occasionally, John attended Elder Nelson's public meetings to guard him against other unruly crowds, and slowly the missionary's message had an effect on John. Some months later, John and his family were baptized. Even though threatening violence is difficult to defend, in this case the fists of the fighter led to the enlightenment of a soul.

Sources

George C. Lambert, comp., *Gems of Reminiscence, Seventeenth Book of the Faith Promoting Series* (Salt Lake City, Utah: Geo. C. Lambert, 1915), 49.

"Gems," 50; Eliza Parkin Dickson and Lynne Dickson Hoffman, *Precious Gems: Parkin, Foulds, Mann, and Busby* (Magna, Utah: The Printing Works, 1981), 29–41.

Alice Walsh Strong: "This I Have Done for Him"

By Andrew Olsen

Lead editor, The Church of Jesus Christ of Latter-day Saints; author of The Price We Paid: The Extraordinary Story of the Willie and Martin Handcart Companies; coauthor of Follow Me to Zion

"Jesus said [that] unless we forsake fathers and mothers, brothers and sisters, houses and lands for His and the gospel's sake, we cannot . . . enter into the kingdom of heaven. This I have done for Him." With these words, handcart pioneer Alice Walsh described some of the sacrifices she made to gather to Zion.

Born in England, Alice was the only member of her parents' family to accept the gospel, joining the Church when she was sixteen. A few years later she married William Walsh, and they emigrated when the handcart plan was introduced in 1856. At the time they had three children, ages four, three, and six months.

The Walsh family became part of the Martin handcart company. Their journey first turned tragic when their oldest son died in Nebraska. A few weeks later, tragedy struck again when Alice's husband died in the area of Devil's Gate,

Wyoming. "The ground was frozen so hard that the men had a difficult task digging the grave deep enough in which to inter him," Alice wrote. "Here I was left a widow with two young children."

Due to weakness and severe weather, the Martin company sought shelter in Martin's Cove, where they endured five frigid days and nights. By the time the weather improved enough for them to continue, only about one-third of them could walk. Wagons had been emptied to provide room for many to ride, but as they filled with people, no one seemed to notice Alice. Her account paints a picture of quiet desperation:

> I was sitting in the snow with my children on my lap, and it seemed that there was no chance for me to ride, but before the last teams had left the camp I was assigned to ride in the commissary wagon, and did so until our arrival in Salt Lake City.

After leaving England full of hope, Alice ached with loneliness at the journey's end: "Arriving in Salt Lake . . . with two children and the clothes I stood up in, were all of my earthly possessions in a strange land, without kin or relatives."

Alice and her two children were taken into the home of Jacob Strong, and Alice and Jacob soon married. Eventually they had three children of their own.

Jacob died in 1872, leaving Alice a widow again at the age of forty-three. She remained a widow the rest of her life—another fifty-two years. Given the difficulties she faced, did Alice think the sacrifices of coming to Zion were worth it? Toward the end of her life, she testified that they were:

> I have always been proud to know that I had the individual courage to accept and embrace

> the faith and join the Church, to which I have ever been steadfast from that day to this.
>
> "Though the sufferings were terrible I passed [through] in the handcart journey across the plains, I am still thankful that the Lord preserved my life and made it possible for me to reach Zion. . . .
>
> "After all that I have endured and passed through, . . . my testimony is that the Gospel of Jesus Christ of Latter Day Saints is true.

The blessings resulting from Alice's sacrifice extended to her posterity and far beyond. During her lifetime, fourteen of her children and grandchildren served missions. One son also served as a patriarch and was the mayor of Farmington, Utah.

Source

"Autobiographical Sketch of Alice Walsh Strong," Church History Library.

Alma Smith

By Mary Jane Woodger
Professor of Church history and doctrine,
Brigham Young University

During the summer of 1838, the Warren and Amanda Smith family emigrated to Missouri, arriving at Hawn's Mill on October 28 before continuing to Far West. Two days later a mob would kill Warren and one of his sons.

At 4 p.m., "a large body of mounted men with faces blackened or painted like Indians rode up yelling and commenced shooting." When the firing ceased, Amanda saw her oldest son, Willard, emerging from the blacksmith shop with his little brother Alma in his arms. "Oh! They have killed my little Alma!" Amanda cried. Willard replied, "Alma is alive but they have killed father and Sardius!"

Eight-year-old Alma's entire hip joint had been shot away. Not knowing what to do, Amanda prayed, "Oh my Heavenly Father, What shall I do? Thou seest my poor wounded boy and knowest my inexperience. Oh, Heavenly Father, direct me what to do!" Amanda later reported that it was as if a voice was directing her to know what to do. She made a lye from ashes, saturated a cloth with it, and put the cloth directly into the wound. She repeatedly saturated the cloth and put it into the hip joint hole with the mashed flesh. Then she was instructed to go to a nearby slippery-elm tree, make a poultice, and fill the wound with it.

Amanda then turned to her little boy and asked, "Alma, my child, [do] you believe that the Lord made your hip?"

"Yes, mother," Alma, replied.

"Well, the Lord can make something there in the place of your hip, don't you believe He can, Alma?" asked his mother.

"Do you think that the Lord can, mother?" inquired Alma.

"Yes, my son," she replied, "He has showed it all to me in a vision."

She then laid Alma on his face and told her little boy, "Now you lay like that, and don't move, and the Lord will make you another hip."

Alma laid on his face for five weeks until he recovered, a flexible gristle having grown in place of the missing joint and socket. As President James E. Faust informs, "The treatment was unusual for that day and time and unheard of now." Forty years later, Amanda reported that Alma had never been the least bit crippled during his life and served as a living miracle of the power of God.

On that new hip Alma Smith would follow his family on their flight to Illinois and then later across the plains to Salt Lake City. Alma Smith would serve numerous missions—all on foot. But that is not the end of the story.

On one of those missions in 1864, he was in company with Elder Lorenzo Snow, sailing by boat from Honolulu to Lahaina. Their boat was overturned, and Elder Snow was drowned. Elder Snow was given a blessing, but still there was no response. It was Alma Smith and Benjamin Cluff who took the Apostle and rolled him facedown over a barrel to expel the water he had swallowed. Still there was no response. The natives standing by gave him up for dead, but the missionaries refused to yield. They knelt and prayed again and then felt impressed to try something most unusual for that day. Taking turns, they blew into Elder Snow's lungs to reinflate them. They kept at it—and then, suddenly, there was a slight wink of an eye followed by a rattle in the throat.

Lorenzo Snow would live, thanks to the same faith and inspiration that had once saved the man who now saved him. When the Lord said, "If ye had faith as a grain of mustard seed . . . nothing shall be impossible to you" (Matthew 17:20), it was a statement less of size and quantity and more of action and attitude.

Sources

Alexander L. Baugh, "A Rare Account of the Haun's Mill Massacre: The Reminiscence of Willard Gilbert Smith," *Missouri Mormon Frontier Foundation Newsletter* nos. 18/19 (Spring/Fall 1998): 1; and R. Scott Lloyd, "Hawn's Mill Massacre: New Insights and Interpretations," *Deseret News Church News*, November 9, 2013.

Jeanine Fry Ricketts, ed., *By Their Fruits: A History and Genealogy of the Fry Family of Wiltshire, England, and Their Descendants* (Salt Lake City, n.p., n.d.), 181–183.

Edward W. Tullidge, *The Women of Mormondom* (New York: Tullidge & Crandall, 1877).

James E. Faust, "The Shield of Faith," *Ensign*, May 2000.

"An Army Moved"

By Glenn Rawson

Writer, producer, and host of the Joseph Smith Papers and History of the Saints television series

Late one fall evening after Heber and Vilate Kimball had retired to their bed, they were awakened suddenly by a sharp knocking at their door. A neighbor, John Greene, stood at the door and bade them come out and see the incredible scenery in the heavens.

They did so. It was a beautiful starlit New England night, so exceptionally clear and brilliant that Heber said later he could have seen to pick up a pin off the ground.

As the little group watched, a white smoke or cloud formed on the eastern horizon and slowly began to rise upward. As it did, it formed itself into a belt spreading across the sky toward the southwest, and it was accompanied by the sound of a rushing mighty wind.

Gradually, the belt flattened out and broadened across into a bow like a rainbow, becoming transparent with a bluish cast and stretching from horizon to horizon.

No sooner had that bow formed than an army of men appeared arising from the east and began marching twelve abreast across the bow toward the west. As Heber said, "In this bow an army moved." As vivid and real as men in the flesh, they marched in the most profound order, every man stepping in the tracks of his leader in perfect synchronization. They were dressed in the full battle gear of nineteenth-century soldiers, all with muskets and bayonets. They were so clear and distinct that Heber and the small group of neighbors could distinguish the features of their faces and hear the jingle of their equipage as they moved.

Shortly, the entire bow from horizon to horizon was crowded and filled with marching men. The sound of the marching reached clearly to the ears of the astonished onlookers.

Heber later described the event this way: "No man could judge of my feelings when I beheld that army of men, as plainly as ever I saw armies of men in the flesh; it seemed as though every hair of my head was alive."

When the celestial army reached the western horizon, it was met by an opposing force, and a battle ensued. The noise of the rush of men and the clash of the arms was distinct and unmistakable. Heber and his friends watched the scene for hours until it gradually disappeared.

Heber's wife, somewhat afraid, turned to one of the older men in the group and asked, "Father Young, what does all this mean?"

"Why, it's one of the signs of the coming of the Son of Man," he replied.

The night this happened was September 22, 1827—the same night that the angel Moroni delivered the plates of the Book of Mormon into the hands of the Prophet Joseph Smith.

Mormon said, "The devil is an enemy unto God and fighteth against him continually" (Moroni 7:12). To know the Book of Mormon is true is to become the devil's enemy.

Sources

Orson F. Whitney, *Life of Heber C. Kimball: An Apostle— The Father and Founder of the British Mission*, 2nd ed. (Salt Lake City, Utah: Bookcraft, 1945), 16–17.

https://books.google.com/books?id=jdkRAAAAIAAJ&pg=PA32&lpg=PA32&dq=%22as+plainly+as+ever+I+saw+armies+of+men+in+the+flesh%22&source=bl&ots=40tCB2rPJw&sig=JB_YUXNDWwUmmuQqONZbMF5kJDY&hl=en&sa=X&ei=K4RnVbPpCIuksAXGyoLABA&ved.

Ann Rowley

By Glenn Rawson

Writer, producer, and host of the Joseph Smith Papers and History of the Saints television series

The year was 1856; Ann Rowley was a widow with a large family living in England. After being baptized a Latter-day Saint, Ann dreamed of going to Zion, where she could be with the Saints. However, money was a problem. It cost more than she could muster to make such a journey, and it took all she had just to care for her large family. Still she was determined. Everyone who could work did, until finally, with the generous help of others, there was enough to make the journey to Utah.

Ann and eight children set sail on the ship *Thornton* in early May 1856 from Liverpool. After arriving in America, they journeyed to the railroad terminus at Iowa City, where the company was outfitted with handcarts and began their journey.

It was August 16, 1856, when the Willie handcart company left Florence, Nebraska, bound for the Salt Lake Valley more than a thousand miles distant. At first the company journeyed in high spirits, but as they moved farther west their spirits began to flag. The handcarts were heavy, and the road was endless, always seeming to climb upward. As for food, there was never enough.

Day after day they walked and pulled the handcart, their strength waning with every step. They grew weaker and weaker until one cherished older daughter finally passed away. Ann described how it hurt to see her children go hungry, cutting strips of rawhide from the cart wheels and chewing them as they walked for a measure of nourishment.

One night somewhere in that vast, cold wilderness, there was no food at all for the evening meal. Ann knelt to pray, and as she did, she remembered two old sea biscuits left over from their ocean voyage weeks earlier. She rummaged through their meager belongings and found the biscuits. They were very hard—so hard, in fact, that they could not be broken—and were so small. "Surely," Ann said, "that was not enough to feed eight people, but five loaves and two fishes were not enough to feed five thousand people either, but through a miracle, Jesus had done it."

She took the two pieces of hardtack, placed them in a Dutch oven, and covered them with water. She asked for God's blessing and placed the pan in the coals. "When I took off the lid a little later," she said, "I found the pan filled with food. I kneeled with my family and thanked God for his goodness. That night my family had sufficient food."

Source

Andrew Olsen, *The Price We Paid: The Extraordinary Story of the Willie and Martin Handcart Pioneers* (2006), 113.

Arthur Parker

By Susan Easton Black
Professor emeritus of Church history and doctrine,
Brigham Young University

In a world where the "love of men shall wax cold" (D&C 45:27), kindness and compassion in any setting are miracles in themselves.

In the late 1850s, European converts pushed their precious possessions in handcarts to the Salt Lake Valley. Among the converts were Robert and Ann Parker and their four children. The Parkers traveled with the first handcart company under the leadership of Daniel Duncan McArthur. They experienced only minor difficulties on the trek until late June 1856, when an unexpected thunderstorm arose and they were asked to quickly set up a makeshift camp. In the process of setting up camp, the Parkers discovered that their six-year-old son, Arthur, was missing. As word spread through the encampment, one pioneer recalled that "earlier in the day, when they had stopped, that they had seen the little boy settle down to rest under the shade of some brush."

For two days, the handcarts remained entrenched in the makeshift camp while the men of the McArthur company searched for the young boy. When Arthur was not found, Captain McArthur, seeing no alternative, ordered the company to move forward. Robert Parker refused to go on without his son. On July 2, 1856, diarist Archer Walters penned, "Brother Parker's little boy, age six, was lost, and the father went back to hunt for him."

Before Robert left to search for his son, Ann "pinned a bright shawl about his shoulders" and said, "If you find him dead, wrap him in the shawl to bury him. If you find him alive, you could use this as a flag to signal us."

As the mother moved on with the other handcart pioneers, Robert continued to search. Miraculously, he found his son in the care of a nameless woodsman. President Boyd K. Packer said of this father and son, "I've often wondered how unlikely it was that a woodsman should be there—found the little boy and described him as being sick with illness and with terror, and he cared for him until his father found him." President Packer also reflected on the plight of the boy's mother: "Out on the trail each night Ann Parker kept watch. At sundown on July 5, as they were watching, they saw a figure approaching from the east! Then, in the rays of the setting sun, she saw the glimmer of the bright red shawl" as the sun was setting.

Archer Walters recorded the return of Robert Parker and his son Arthur: "Brother Parker came into camp with a little boy that had been lost. Great joy through the camp. The mother's joy I cannot describe." Another diarist recorded, "Ann Parker fell in a pitiful heap upon the sand, and that night, for the first time in six nights, she slept."

Sources

LeRoy R. Hafen and Ann W. Hafen, *Handcarts to Zion, The Story of a Unique Western Migration 1856–1860 with Contemporary Journals, Accounts, Reports, and Rosters of Members of the Ten Handcart Companies* (Glendale, CA: Arthur H. Clark Co., 1960), 61.

Kate B. Carter, *Treasures of Pioneer History* (Salt Lake City, Utah: Daughters of Utah Pioneers), 5:240–241.

Boyd K. Packer, "Where Much Is Given, Much Is Required," *Ensign*, Nov. 1974, 89–90.

At Cumorah

By Glenn Rawson

STORYTELLER ON THE *SOUNDS OF SUNDAY* RADIO PROGRAM

MONDAY MORNING, SEPTEMBER 22, 1823, seventeen-year-old Joseph Smith Jr. climbed up the forested west face of a hill later to be called Cumorah. The night previous, Joseph had been visited by an angel who had told him of an ancient record buried in that hill and who had showed him by vision the exact place. Joseph now stood before a large stone that covered that record. The stone was too heavy to lift, so Joseph found a lever and "with a little exertion raised it up." Under the stone was a box formed of stones and mortared together with cement. Inside the box was an ancient record written on gold plates giving an account of the former inhabitants of the Americas.

"On attempting to take possession of the record a shock was produced upon his system, by an invisible power which deprived him, in a measure, of his natural strength. He . . . made another attempt, but was more sensibly shocked than before."

Calculating that he needed to try harder, he reached again. "When his strength failed him more than at either of the former times . . . he exclaimed, 'Why can I not obtain this book?'"

From nearby came a voice, "Because you have not kept the commandments of the Lord." It was the angel of the Lord.

Joseph had been warned that he must have no other object in view of getting the plates than to glorify God. He realized that in his thoughts he had been "tempted of the adversary and sought the plates to obtain riches."

Humbled, Joseph prayed. "The heavens were opened and the glory of the Lord shone round about, and rested upon him. While he thus stood gazing and admiring, the angel said, 'Look!' and, as he thus spake, he beheld the prince of darkness, surrounded by his innumerable train of associates. All this passed before him, and the heavenly messenger said, 'All this is shown, the good and the evil, the holy and impure, the glory of God and the power of darkness, that you may know hereafter the two powers and never be influenced or overcome by that wicked one.'"

One year later, on September 22, 1824, "Joseph again visited the place where he found the plates the year previous. . . . He fully expected to carry them home with him." He removed the plates from the box and then, thinking there might be something else in the box of value, he set the plates down, turned back, and carefully covered the box again. "He turned [around] to take the Record again, but . . . it was gone. . . . He was much alarmed. He kneeled down and asked the Lord why the Record had been taken from him." Once again, the angel appeared and reminded him that "he had been commanded not to lay the plates down."

He was permitted to open the box again. Upon seeing the plates once more inside the box, he reached for them, but "was hurled back upon the ground with great violence." Joseph returned home weeping with disappointment, "aware that [his family] would expect him to bring the Plates home with him."

The commandments of God are strict. It is not enough for any of us to be willing to keep the commandments of God. We must practice obedience until, by the grace of God, we are obedient.

On September 22, 1825, Joseph returned again to the hill, but we have no account of what happened.

Then, in September of 1826, Joseph returned to the hill and met the angel. He asked for the record but was told that this was not the year, but, "If he would do right according to the will of God he might obtain it on the 22nd of September next, and if not he never would have them." The angel also added that he "might have the book if he brought with him the right person." When Joseph asked who that right person was, he was told that he would know. That person was later revealed to be Emma Hale.

Just after midnight on September 22, 1827, Joseph and Emma Smith, now married, returned to the hill. Emma stayed with the carriage while Joseph climbed the hill and took up the record. "The angel of the Lord stood by and said, Now you have got the record into your own hands, and you are but a man, therefore you will have to be watchful and faithful to your trust, or you will be overpowered by wicked men. . . . Beware, and look well to your ways, and you shall have power to retain it, until the time for it to be translated."

Praise God that Joseph succeeded! The voice of the ancients speaking out of the ground, low out of the dust, is now whispering out of the dust to men once more (see Isaiah 29).

Sources

Joseph Smith History, 1832.

Messenger and Advocate, 2:198.

Lucy Mack Smith, *History of Joseph Smith by His Mother* (Salt Lake City, Utah: Deseret Book, 2009), 83–84.

Joseph Knight Sr. Recollection.

Back to Life

By Mark Ogletree
Associate professor of Church history and doctrine,
Brigham Young University

A young woman in Salina, Utah, had become very ill and was close to death. A neighbor sought out Ephraim Hanks to heal her:

> [Ephraim] arrived in Salina very late in the afternoon. As he rode into the yard of the dying woman, her husband came out to meet them. The husband said, "You're too late. She died a couple of hours ago. The Relief Society Sisters are preparing the body now."
>
> Eph asked, "Who gave them the order to commission her unto death?" He then . . . plunged his head into the horse trough all the way down, . . . went over to his saddle, took off a burlap sack and dried his hair and beard . . . and went into the house. . . . He then ordered those women to cover the body and leave the room. There were protests, but his cold, calm look left no

> doubt in their minds that they were to depart. . . . It was about two hours later when Ephraim came out from the room looking very tired. Closing the door behind him, he quietly told her husband, "Your wife is sitting up in bed and would like to talk to you." . . .
>
> Ephraim was never one to stand in front of a miracle he performed seeking the praise of others. Whenever he performed these miracles he just drifted out of sight and returned to his home.
>
> The husband went into the bedroom finding his wife sitting up in bed. On seeing him she exclaimed, "I dozed off and took a nap. Now how long have I slept?" Mr. Johnson replied, "You have been a very sick woman for ten days. We thought we were going to lose you."
>
> Mr. Johnson's wife replied, "I had the most wonderful dream. I dreamed there was a man with long-flowing white hair and a full-flowing white beard sitting here beside my bed, holding my hand. He told me that I would bear and raise seven daughters. The man also said there would be a time in life when they would all stand together and be a great joy to me."
>
> Sister Johnson did live to raise seven daughters and there was a time when each of them was either ward or stake Relief Society presidents concurrently.

Indeed, "the rights of the Priesthood are inseparably connected with the powers of heaven, and . . . cannot be controlled nor handled only upon the principles of righteousness" (D&C 121:36), but when there is righteousness and meekness, there is no limit to the good that a man can do.

Source

J. Phillip Hanks, *I Am Ready Now: The Life Story of Ephraim Knowlton Hanks* (Provo, Utah: Brigham Young University Press, 2013), 158–159.

"Be Still, and Know That I Am God"

By Matthew C. Godfrey

MANAGING HISTORIAN, *JOSEPH SMITH PAPERS*

IN JULY 1831, JOSEPH SMITH received a revelation declaring that Jackson County, Missouri, was the location of the City of Zion. The revelation also commanded Church leaders such as Edward Partridge and William W. Phelps to plant themselves in Jackson County—specifically Independence—so that they could lead the development of the city there.

For the next two years, Partridge—one of two bishops in the Church—purchased land, and Church members migrated to the area to settle. They fully expected that once they built the city and constructed a temple in it, Jesus Christ would return to the earth, ushering in the Millennium.

But it was not to be. In the summer of 1833, fearing that the Saints were overwhelming the non-Mormon population in Jackson County and upset at an editorial written by Phelps in the Church's newspaper, a group of Missourians destroyed the Church's printing office, tarred and feathered Partridge, and demanded that all Saints evacuate the county—half by January 1, 1834, and the rest by April 1834. Church leaders agreed to these terms, but once they sought legal counsel as to how to obtain redress for the attacks, the Missourians struck again, driving the Saints from the county in the first week of November 1833. Zion, it seemed, was lost.

After receiving information from Oliver Cowdery and other Missouri Church leaders about the expulsion, Joseph Smith was troubled, wondering why these afflictions had come upon the Saints and how Zion would be redeemed. As he pondered these questions, no answers seemed forthcoming: the heavens were shut. On December 10, 1833, he wrote to Bishop Partridge and other Church leaders:

> There are two things of which I am ignorant and the Lord will not show me—perhaps for a wise purpose in himself. . . . and they are these, Why God hath suffered so great calamity to come upon Zion; or what the great moving cause of this great affliction is. . . . and again by what means he will return her back to her inheritance with songs of everlasting joy upon her head.

When he inquired about these things, Joseph said, "the voice of the Lord is, Be still, and know that I am God." Six days later, as Joseph and Oliver sat together in the evening, the answers finally came. Joseph received what is now section 101 of the Doctrine and Covenants, specifically telling him why the Lord allowed the Saints to be driven from Jackson County and how Zion would be redeemed.

How often in our own lives do we seek the Lord only to feel that the heavens are silent? On such occasions, we would do well to remember that even the Prophet Joseph experienced such times. But he trusted in God and the answers eventually came. At such times, we too should follow the Lord's counsel to Joseph: "Be still, and know that I am God."

Sources

Revelation, 20 July 1831 [D&C 57], in Matthew C. Godfrey, Mark Ashurst-McGee, Grant Underwood, Robert J. Woodford, and William G. Hartley, eds., *Documents, Volume 2: July 1831–January 1833*, vol. 2 of the Documents series of *The Joseph Smith Papers*, ed. Dean C. Jessee, Ronald K. Esplin, and Richard Lyman Bushman (Salt Lake City, Utah: Church Historian's Press, 2013), 5–12.

Revelation, 16–17 December 1833 [D&C 101], in Gerrit J. Dirkmaat, Brent M. Rogers, Grant Underwood, Robert J. Woodford, and William G. Hartley, eds., *Documents, Volume 3: February 1833–March 1834*, vol. 3 of the Documents series of *The Joseph Smith Papers*, ed. Ronald K. Esplin and Matthew J. Grow (Salt Lake City, Utah: Church Historian's Press, 2014), 386–397.

Letter to Edward Partridge and Others, 10 December 1833, in *Documents, Volume 3*, 375–381.

Besting the Waves: The Dream

By Glenn Rawson

WRITER, PRODUCER, AND HOST OF THE *JOSEPH SMITH PAPERS* AND *HISTORY OF THE SAINTS* TELEVISION SERIES

A MAN ONCE HAD A dream where he found himself "standing on a peninsula in the midst of a vast body of water where there appeared to be a large harbor or pier for boats to come to." He was surrounded by his friends.

Presently a strong wind came up that increased into a raging storm, making the waters very rough. A ship began to leave the harbor and make its way "out into the channel." The man turned to his friends and warned them "that if they did not understand the Signs of the Times and the Spirit of Prophecy, they would be apt to be lost." Within moments, they witnessed the violent waves break over the departing ship. It "soon foundered and went down with all on board."

The man declared to his friends that he believed he could best those waves and beat the storm. They laughed at him and said he would drown.

"The waters looked clear and beautiful" he said, "though exceedingly rough; and I said I believed I could swim, and I would try it anyhow." They told him again he would drown. He decided that if he was going to drown, then he would have fun in the water first, and with that he dove into the "raging waves."

He had not gone far when a towering wave overwhelmed him, but he soon found himself on top of it. Then another wave broke over him and he topped it also. "I struggled hard," he said, "to live in the midst of the storm and waves, and soon found I gained upon every wave and skimmed the torrent better." Shortly he discovered that he was able to swim with his head above the waves so that they could not break over him.

He had swum a great distance and found that he was enjoying himself a great deal. He became stronger and faster until both his head and shoulders were above the water, and he was faster than any ship. The water seemed to calm. His body rose higher and higher until "finally [he] could tread on the top of the water, and went almost with the speed of an arrow." He thought "it was a great sport and pleasure to travel with such speed." Then he awoke.

The man who experienced that significant dream was Joseph Smith. In that dream, Joseph mentions that his brother Samuel was in the water with him and also bested the waves to tread on top of the water. The date this dream was related by Joseph to Wilford Woodruff, W. W. Phelps, and Willard Richards, was February 2, 1844—just five months before Joseph and Samuel would die a martyr's death.

John the Revelator wrote, "To him that overcometh will I grant to sit with me in my throne, even as I also overcame, and am set down with my Father in his throne" (Revelation 3:5). By the grace of God, so may all men overcome.

Sources

History of the Church, 6:194.
Journal History of the Church, February 2, 1844.

"Better to Live on Raw Carrots"

By Steven M. Parkin

Civil Engineer

From my desk today in Salt Lake, I sometimes read transcripts of journals of my ancestral grandfathers. As I read, a story unfolds as if I were present. Two ancestors, John Parkin and his son William of Loscoe, Derbyshire, England, told a story that was transforming to me.

After joining the Church in England, John moved to America in 1863, migrating to South Bountiful, Utah, where he supported his family as a carrot farmer. At harvest one year, father and son drove their wagon full of carrots to Salt Lake to sell at market, intending to return home before it got dark. Along a street, they happened upon a longtime Church member, known in William's journal only as Brother T, a man of wealth and thrift in the Salt Lake community. Brother T was a former missionary who traveled Derbyshire and frequently visited the Parkin family.

Upon meeting, they discussed the carrots and agreed on twenty-five cents per bushel. After some negotiating, Brother T decided to buy all forty bushels. After they drove the wagon into his yard, Brother T brought a bushel basket for measuring, not trusting John's prior estimated measurement. Knowing that he had generously estimated the content, John had no objection, but did regret the delay in returning home before dark.

With the wagon half unloaded, Brother T was called by his wife to dinner; he asked his old acquaintances to wait for him while he ate his supper. Work was suspended; father and son reflected while they waited. Their appetites were keen enough to enjoy a good dinner but it was not offered.

While waiting, John said, "My son, can you imagine Elder T when he was a missionary in England eating carrots in a barn while I indulged in a warm meal in the house?"

"On the contrary," the son said to his father. "I remember distinctly that he never called at our house without being invited to eat . . . and that the choicest cuts of meat were brought to provide him the best meal possible." Moreover, "that you paid thirty-six shillings for silk," the son added, "to make a pair of stockings as a gift for his wife" when he returned home.

"Yes," John responded. "When I embraced Mormonism, I did it because I was sure it was the truth, and I afterwards tried to serve the Lord just as thoroughly as I had ever served the devil." Before his conversion, John had been an irreligious man who didn't believe in prayer and had no regard for sacred things. Rather, he had been a street fighter who loved a good scrap.

"Brother T probably knows that the Gospel is true, but it has apparently not changed his nature," the father told his son. "I don't envy him, his nature or his possessions," he added. "Better live on raw carrots and retain our love for the truth . . . than have the wealth of this world." William knew well of the miracle that had changed his father.

Brother T returned from the house and the count resumed. When there were only a few bushels left, he exclaimed: "Never mind measuring any more, I see you have forty bushels."

William interrupted, "We will finish measuring." There were forty-two bushels, and Brother T. "shamefacedly handed over $10.50."

This is what it means to be changed in the inner man—to "have a mighty change wrought in us or in our hearts, that we have no more disposition to do evil, but to do good continually" (Mosiah 5:2).

Sources

Eliza Parkin Dickson and Lynne Dickson Hoffman, *Precious Gems: Parkin, Foulds, Mann and Busby* (Magna, Utah: The Printing Werks, 1981), 40, 41.

George C. Lambert, comp., *Gems of Reminiscence, Seventeenth Book of the Faith-Promoting Series* (Salt Lake City, Utah: Geo. C. Lambert, 1915), 53–54.

"Blessed of the Lord": Emma Smith's Patriarchal Blessing

By Matthew C. Godfrey

Managing historian, *Joseph Smith Papers*

Emma Hale Smith was a woman who experienced much tribulation in her life. In the first several years after marrying the Prophet Joseph Smith in 1827, Emma gave birth to three children, all of whom died just hours after birth. After the death of twins in April 1831, Emma and Joseph adopted the Murdock twins—babies whose mother, Julia Murdock, had just died in childbirth. The twins provided much joy to Emma and Joseph, but when they were eleven months old, one of them—Joseph Murdock, who had been suffering from measles—perished after being exposed to the cold night air when a mob ripped the Prophet from his bed in Hiram, Ohio, to be tarred and feathered.

In the course of about four years, then, Emma and Joseph had seen four of their children die. Although death was perhaps a more familiar thing to early-nineteenth-century Americans, these losses still hurt. As Joseph told Emma upon hearing that his brother Hyrum's nearly three-year-old daughter had died in 1832, "I think we can in some degree sympathize with him."

Given this backdrop, a blessing that Emma received from her father-in-law, Joseph Smith Sr., on December 9, 1834, was especially significant. In December 1834, Joseph Smith Sr. was designated as a Patriarch to the Church. He began to fulfill his calling by gathering his children and their spouses for a special feast on December 9 and then blessing each of them. When he got to Emma, he told her that she was "blessed of the Lord, for thy faithfulness and truth" and stated that she would "rejoice in the glory" that her husband Joseph would obtain. Then he spoke to her about her "pure desires to raise up a family," telling her that she had "seen much sorrow because the Lord has taken from thee three of thy children." However, if she continued to have faith, God would bless her with "other children, to the joy and satisfaction of thy soul, and to the rejoicing of thy friends."

Although there is no record of what Emma thought of this blessing, such words must have been of great comfort. As the years passed, they proved prophetic. At the time of the blessing, Emma and Joseph had two children: Julia Murdock—the surviving twin—and Joseph Smith III, born in 1832. After the blessing, they had three more children who grew to adulthood: Frederick Granger Williams Smith, born in 1836; Alexander Hale Smith, born in 1838; and David Hyrum Smith, born in 1844. The promise made to her by her father-in-law was fulfilled, and Emma truly rejoiced in her children.

"Whether by mine own voice or by the voice of my servants, it is the same" (D&C 1:38).

Source

Blessing from Joseph Smith Sr., Dec. 9, 1834, http://josephsmithpapers.org/paperSummary/blessing-from-joseph-smith-sr-9-december-1834.

Born Deaf and Dumb

By William G. Hartley

RETIRED PROFESSOR OF HISTORY, BRIGHAM YOUNG UNIVERSITY

IN ROCHDALE, ENGLAND, ON MARCH 25, 1854, Mormon missionaries John S. Fullmer and David B. Dille met with four people who wanted to be baptized: Mrs. Howarth, her son and daughter, and her brother. Her brother, age eighteen, had been born deaf and dumb. Mrs. Howarth assured the elders that she had instructed her brother and that he could read well and that he conversed fluently by writing.

Elder Dille, wanting to be sure that the young man was ready for baptism, wrote on a slate: "Do you want to be baptized for the remission of your sins? If so, please answer." The lad asked his sister the meaning of remission. She replied it was forgiveness. He then wrote, "Yes."

Both elders simultaneously felt impressed that the young man would receive his hearing and his speech, and said so to each other.

After Elder Dille baptized the four, all returned to a home for the confirmations. "I felt to ask God, while our hands were upon the young man's head," Elder Fullmer said, "that he might be made to hear and speak. We then told his sister, that if she would come again with her brother in the morning, we would anoint him for his hearing."

In a report to mission president Samuel W. Richards, Elder Fullmer told in detail about what then transpired. He said that the next morning the elders anointed the young man with consecrated oil. "I gave him a little inwardly, that it might touch his tongue," Elder Fullmer said, "applied some also about his ears, and dropped some into them, in the name of the Lord, praying that the young man might be blessed with hearing and with speech." Then he and Elder Dille "laid our hands upon his head."

But Elder Fullmer sensed that Elder Dille "did not speak with that confidence which is void of doubt—he said nothing positive." Elder Fullmer felt "a little disappointed in my spirit." He reflected a few minutes and then realized that "we ought to act in our official capacity 'as men having authority.'" He said, "for to this end we were called and sent; and that in places where there were none over us in authority, we must officiate instead of and for God, on the earth." He expressed those feelings out loud and asserted that "we ought to command every obstacle to his hearing and speaking, to depart from him, in the name of the Lord." Elder Dille assented.

So the elders again laid hands upon the young man, and Elder Fullmer "rebuked every obstruction to his hearing and speech, in the name of the Lord Jesus Christ, and commanded the same to depart from him, so that he should have the power of both speech and hearing given unto him, and said, this should be his blessing; if he would receive it in faith, for a testimony to him, and to all who were acquainted with him."

The young man's sister communicated to him what the elders had sealed upon him if he would believe. "He rejoiced greatly, and it was manifest to all, that the Spirit rested greatly upon him," Elder Fullmer recorded. "He said that he did believe, by sticking up his thumb, which meant anything that was good. He also communicated that we were men of God. He opened the

Bible at the last chapter of St. Mark, and pointed to the words of the Saviour to the Apostles, and the promise to them that believed and were baptized, that these signs should follow them."

The group went to the sister's house and conversed concerning the young man. Then Elder Fullmer saw something remarkable happen:

> I discovered about an hour after the administration of the oil, that he manifested signs of hearing. I removed from his ears the cotton which I had applied after the oil, and requested his sister to read the alphabet to him on the hand, and at the same time to speak the letters. He was requested to observe the movement of her lips and tongue, and to imitate her in the sound. We then learned, to our great joy, that he could actually hear, and, as he was directed, to follow his sister in sounding every letter in the alphabet, many of them quite distinctly.

The young man repeated the words father, mother, brother, sister, his own name, Elder Dille's and Elder Fullmer's names, and many other words. He was exceedingly delighted at what was happening. His hearing appeared to become gradually more distinct, so that he satisfactorily heard words spoken with the usual strength of voice when directed clearly to him. Everyone praised him "till he made us understand that his lungs were tired. We dismissed him for that time. I instructed his sister to give him frequent lessons."

His younger brother was much astonished. He said his brother had never talked before, and now he knew that what the elders preached was verily true, and that he was ready to obey the gospel and be baptized. "So we baptized him the self-same hour. And we all rejoiced greatly in the Lord our God."

Jesus promised, "He that believeth on me, the works that I do shall he do also; and greater works that these shall he do; because I go unto my Father" (John 14:12), and so it has come to pass.

Source

John S. Fullmer to Dear President S. W. Richards, April 16, 1854, published as "Remarkable Manifestation of the Power of God," *Millennial Star* 16 (May 6, 1854), 283–284.

Carrying On

By Glenn Rawson

Writer, producer, and host of the *Joseph Smith Papers* and *History of the Saints* television series

After the death of her beloved husband, Eliza was "prostrated with grief and besought the Lord with all the fervency of her soul to permit her to follow" her husband to the grave immediately, "and not leave her in so dark and wicked a world. And so set was her mind on the matter that she did not and could not cease that prayer of her heart."

And then, from beyond the veil, her husband appeared to her and "told her that she must not continue to supplicate the Lord in that way, for her petition was not in accordance with his design concerning her. [He] told her that his work upon earth was completed as far as the mortal tabernacle was concerned, but her work was not. The Lord desired her, and so did her husband, to live many years, and assist in carrying on the great Latter-day work." She was admonished to "be of good courage and help to cheer, and lighten the burdens of others. And that she must turn her thoughts away from her own loneliness, and seek to console her people in their bereavement and sorrow."

Eliza obediently got up off her knees and went to work. When the Saints left Nauvoo in 1846, bound for the Rocky Mountains, Eliza went with them. As the Saints suffered and struggled at Winter Quarters, Nebraska, Eliza was there lifting, teaching, and comforting. Across the plains in 1847, she carried the original minutes of the Relief Society, fording rivers and braving storms. In Salt Lake City, she stood with Brigham Young, loyal to his leadership and fierce in her defense of the work.

In 1866, at the request of Brigham Young, she went throughout the territory organizing the women into ward Relief Societies, and in 1880 she was called as the second general president of the Relief Society. She would gain renown as one of the most influential women of the nineteenth century. She would become known as Zion's Poetess, and through such poems as "O My Father," she would administer comfort and joy to her people even down to the present day.

Who was she—who was the woman overcome with grief who prayed to die in the summer of 1844? She was Eliza R. Snow—the plural wife of Joseph Smith.

Nephi said, "Yea, my God will give me, if I ask not amiss; therefore I will lift up my voice unto thee" (2 Nephi 4:35). We must remember that it is not enough to pray fervently; we must also pray wisely.

Source

Andrew M. Jenson, *Latter-day Saints Biographical Encyclopedia: Compilation of Biographical Sketches of Prominent Men and Women in the Church of Jesus Christ of Latter-day Saints*, 4 vols. (Salt Lake City, Utah: Andrew Jenson History Co., 1901), 1:695.

Feramorz Little Young

By Glenn Rawson

STORYTELLER ON THE *SOUNDS OF SUNDAY* RADIO PROGRAM

FERAMORZ LITTLE YOUNG WAS AN exceptional young man. He was born September 16, 1856, in Salt Lake City to Brigham and Lucy Decker Young. He was the sixth of seven children born to the couple and grew up in the Beehive House. He attended school at the University of Deseret and then at age sixteen he entered the United States Naval Academy. By age twenty-one he had graduated from the Troy Polytechnic Institute. As a student he excelled.

As a Latter-day Saint he was a stripling son of courage, defended the faith constantly during his time in the East. Then on November 16, 1880, Fera Young left Salt Lake City to serve as a missionary in Mexico City. His diary is filled with those entries typical of any young man serving as a missionary.

Toward the end of his mission he began to feel unwell. Along with Elder Moses Thatcher, Elder Young began his journey for home. While at sea Fera grew worse and began to sense that he was not going to live. Finally, on September 27, 1881, just off the coast of Havana, Cuba, Elder Feramorz Young passed away and was buried at sea.

His passing was a great trial to Elder Thatcher and also to his family and friends. How could such a pure and intelligent young man, capable of doing so much good, be called home? What a terrible loss. His mother would say of him that she "could not remember a word, thought or act of his life that would bring her the least sorrow or uneasiness." Fera's closest boyhood friend, would later say of him, "if ever there was a clean, sweet, absolutely pure young man upon the earth he was that young man."

And in most instances, the story tragically ends there—but not this time.

Years later a woman—not a Latter-day Saint, a stranger—came to the home of Lucy Decker Young and related the following story to Fera's mother:

> Now Mrs. Young, I do not believe a thing of what I am going to tell you. This girl friend of mine was one of the noblest, finest, choicest kind of girls and young women that ever lived. She has come to me in this city of Salt Lake on three separate occasions at night in dreams, and has given me this information: the date of her birth, the date of her death, and all that is necessary, she says, for a record in the Temple: and she has told me that your son, Feramorz L. Young has converted her and that in addition to converting her he has proposed marriage to her.

The young woman then commanded her doubting friend to go to Sister Young and tell her the story and vouch for her virtue and integrity. This young woman had not grown up in Salt Lake City and this woman was the only one who knew her and could vouch for the uprightness of her life. The young woman requested that her work be done and that she be married by proxy to Fera.

The woman said again to Mother Young, "I do not believe a word of it." But then she seemed to plead for Sister Young to do something, because she said, "The last time this young woman came to me she said, 'You might just as well go to Mrs. Young and give her this information, because I am going to come and come and come until you do it.'"

The woman then said, "I just cannot bear to have her come again."

In February 1931, President Heber J. Grant said of the situation, "This beautiful girl was sealed to Brother Young, and I am convinced that my dear friend lost nothing by dying in his youth."

Sources

https://archive.org/stream/improvementera3404unse#page/n6/mode/1up

https://lib.byu.edu/collections/mormon-missionary-diaries/about/diarists/feramorz-little-young/

Conversion of Brigham Young

By Glenn Rawson

STORYTELLER ON THE *SOUNDS OF SUNDAY* RADIO PROGRAM

THEY WERE A TYPICAL LARGE New England family: very poor—so poor, in fact, that the children were not afforded the luxury of an education. The only learning they received came in the form of hard work on the farm.

The parents were "some of the most strict religionists upon the earth." To violate the family's religious standards would bring forth swift paternal discipline. Mother was of a more gentle approach and was revered by her children. She encouraged them to "do everything that is good; do nothing that is evil; and if you see any persons in distress administer to their wants."

But then tuberculosis claimed their mother, Nabby Young, resulting in the family being broken up and scattered. When he was only sixteen years old, Nabby and John Young's ninth son, Brigham, left home to make his way in the world.

About this time Brigham's brother Lorenzo had a dream in which he saw a gold carriage drawn by a beautiful pair of white horses. The Savior was in that carriage. When it stopped before Lorenzo, "the Savior inquired, 'Where is your brother

Brigham?' After answering his question He inquired about my other brothers, and concerning my father. . . . He stated that he wanted us all, but especially my brother Brigham."

Brigham matured and became a skilled and conscientious craftsmen. When he was twenty-three he married Miriam Works, who was described as a "beautiful blond with blue eyes and wavy hair; gentle and lovable." Together they had two children, Elizabeth and Vilate.

Brigham Young was fiercely independent. Though he never drank, when members of his family urged him to sign a temperance pledge, he refused, saying "I wish to do just right, without being bound to do it; I want my liberty. My independence is sacred to me."

This sense of independence carried over into religion. He developed his own ideas of God and the scriptures. Amidst the fervor of revivalism, he remained skeptical of churches. They were empty to him. He wanted to know God and how to find Him, but none could answer his questions. Angry ministers called him an infidel.

It was September 1827 when Brigham saw a marvelous vision in the heavens of warring armies. He would remember it all his days and consider it a sign. Yet Brigham became discouraged. His questions remained unanswered, his quest unfulfilled.

Then the Book of Mormon came into the family. Father, brothers, sisters, and relatives all embraced it quickly, but not Brigham. He was leery of being taken in. For eighteen months he pondered the book, compared its teachings to the Bible, and scrutinized those who believed in it. It was not enough to feel or believe it was true; he had to know. Then came the day when Eleazar Miller bore humble testimony to the truth of the Restoration, and Brigham's soul was filled with light and certainty. He was baptized April 14, 1832. Miriam would follow three weeks later.

Brigham was reborn. "I wanted to thunder and roar out the Gospel to the nations," he said. "It burned in my bones like fire pent up." And preach the gospel he did, but he could never go far from home. Miriam had contracted tuberculosis and was slipping away. Each day Brigham "got breakfast for his wife, himself, and the little girls, dressed the children, cleaned up the house, carried his wife to the rocking chair by the fireplace and left her there until he could return in the evening. When he came home he cooked his own and the family's supper, put his wife back to bed and finished up the day's domestic labors."

In September 1832, Miriam Young passed away, she and Brigham confident they would be together again forever. With his wife gone and his daughters under the motherly watchcare of Vilate Kimball, Brigham Young closed his shop, gave away his earthly possessions, and set out to preach the gospel that seemed like a fire in his bones.

Source

Ronald K. Esplin, "Conversion and Transformation: Brigham Young's New York Roots and the Search for Bible Religion," *Regional Studies in Latter-day Saint Church History*, 1992, 165–201.

Cyclone of '78

By Glenn Rawson

Writer, producer, and host of the *Joseph Smith Papers* and *History of the Saints* television series

It was June 1878. All was quiet and peaceful until suddenly, from nowhere, a tornado swept down on the unsuspecting village of Richmond, Missouri. It ripped through the community with a devastating swathe, destroying one-third of the city. *The Ray Chronicle* reported the news as follows:

> Language is too poor to adequately describe the desolation and ruin of Richmond. Within a few moments a third of the town was made desolate. Five hundred persons made homeless with many of them left penniless. Richmond is in grief and mourning. We have buried twelve bodies of our good citizens.

Another paper described the destruction this way: "The havoc and desolation which then ensued are beyond our abilities to describe. Not a house is left to mark that once beautiful portion of the town. . . . Nor is there a single foundation that was not swept away." Among those structures destroyed was the county courthouse. Witnesses later declared that books from the courthouse were found forty miles away in the aftermath of the storm.

David and his family lived at 213 East Main Street and were among those affected by what they called "the cyclone." *The Ray Chronicle* reported that David's home—a two-story, seven-room structure built in 1843—was "torn to atoms" when the house across the street was blown through it. David himself was injured by flying timbers. It was a fact noted throughout the community and spread far and wide that, through it all, one small room of David's house was unaffected by the killer storm. Though the rest of the house was destroyed, nothing in the room was disturbed; the entire room was intact. Not even the windows were broken.

For the rest of his life, David and his family would assert that it was divine providence that protected that room and its contents.

What was in that room? The printer's manuscript of the Book of Mormon. And the homeowner was David Whitmer, one of the Three Witnesses of the Book of Mormon.

Like the ark of the covenant anciently and the gold plates in Joseph's day, there are essential artifacts of faith that the Lord will protect for the good of all mankind.

Sources

The Ray Chronicle, June 3, 1878.

"The Town of Richmond, Mo., visited by a Tornado," *Phelps County New Era*, June 8, 1878.

John Hart Interview with David Whitmer, 1883.

http://rsc.byu.edu/archived/joseph-f-smith-reflections-man-and-his-times/excavating-early-mormon-history-1878-history.

Dirty Little Irish Kid

By Glenn Rawson

STORYTELLER ON THE *SOUNDS OF SUNDAY* RADIO PROGRAM

THE YEAR WAS 1875. Two missionaries serving in Liverpool, England, happened to be walking home one night when they noticed a young boy standing on a bridge. Thinking he was too young to be out so late, they offered to walk him home. The offer was accepted, and the missionaries walked him to his humble home where they met his mother, Susannah Callis, a widow with four small children who was living in terrible poverty.

The missionaries and their message were accepted and the family joined the Church. Later that same year with the help of the Perpetual Emigrating Fund, the family left England and came to Utah, where they continued to struggle for their survival.

The missionary who baptized the little boy he'd found on the bridge soon completed his mission, and when reporting his labors was heard to say, "Brothers and sisters, I think my mission has been a failure. I've labored all my days as a missionary here and I've only baptized one dirty little Irish kid."

The missionary returned and made his home somewhere in Montana. Many years passed. Sometime after the year 1933, this former missionary, now an old man, heard a knock at his door. When he opened it up, there stood on the threshold a distinguished-looking visitor—a small man, only about five-foot-five, but one with a commanding voice and presence.

The visitor asked if he were Elder so-and-so. The man confirmed that he was.

The visitor then asked, "Do you remember having said that you thought your mission was a failure because you had only baptized one dirty little Irish kid?"

The former missionary nodded.

The visitor then stuck out his hand and said, "I would like to shake hands with you. My name is Charles A. Callis, of the Council of the Twelve [Apostles]. I am that dirty little Irish kid."

What that missionary could not have known in 1875 was that that dirty little Irish kid would grow to become not only an Apostle but one of the greatest missionaries of the twentieth century.

When the Lord commanded that we be "anxiously engaged in a good cause and do many things of [our] own free will, and bring to pass much righteousness" (D&C 58:27), He didn't promise that we would always know the good that would come of it. Sometimes we just never know the good one simple act can cause.

Sources

Harold B. Lee, "Feet Shod with the Preparation of the Gospel of Peace," *Brigham Young University Speeches of the Year* (Provo, Utah: Nov. 9, 1954), 1.

"Chance Meeting of Elders, Irish Lad Leads to Conversion," *Church News*, Oct. 7, 1961, 20

Richard E. Bennett, "Elder Charles A. Callis: Twentieth-Century Missionary," *Ensign*, Apr. 1981, 46.

Eli H. Pierce

By Mark D. Ogletree
Associate professor of Church history and doctrine,
Brigham Young University

On October 5, 1875, Eli Pierce was sitting in a railroad telegraph office smoking an old Dutch pipe and reading a novel. Though a Latter-day Saint, he was not attending the semiannual general conference of the Church because, as he said, "I did not care to be."

Eli was not a church-goer. He smoked cigars; in fact, he said, he bought them by the thousands. He gambled, swore, and drank. He had scarcely read a dozen chapters of scripture in his life and had never preached a public discourse. "Nature," Eli said of himself, "never endowed me with a super-abundance of religious sentiment or veneration." It seems that was an understatement.

All of that notwithstanding, one of Eli's friends was attending conference and heard Eli's name read from the pulpit. Eli was being called to serve as a missionary in the eastern United States. The man ran out and immediately sent Eli a telegraph with the news. When Eli received the telegraph, his first thoughts were, "I marveled and wondered if the Church [was] not running short of missionary material."

What he did next is truly remarkable. "As soon as I had been informed of what had taken place, I threw the novel in the waste basket, the pipe in a corner and started up town to buy [scriptures], [and] have never read a novel nor smoked a pipe from that hour. [I] sent in my resignation . . . to take effect at once, in order that I might have time for study and preparation."

And then Eli records this:

> Remarkable as it may seem, and has since appeared to me, a thought of disregarding the call, or of refusing to comply with the requirement, never once entered my mind. The only question I asked—and I asked it a thousand times—was: How can I accomplish this mission? How can I, who am so shamefully ignorant and untaught in doctrine, do honor to God and justice to the souls of men, and merit the trust reposed in me by the Priesthood?

Determined to serve, Eli was mocked by some of his friends. They said he would not last six months.

They were wrong.

Eli arrived in Pennsylvania and went to work. At first he did all he could to avoid speaking in public, but in time things changed. Speaking of him and his companion, he wrote, "Through prayerfulness, humility, and persevering faith, we soon obtained the coveted testimony, [and] were greatly blessed of the Lord in freedom of speech and delivery, and we became known in that locality as 'the boy evangelists.'"

It was on that mission that Elder Pierce had a remarkable experience. He was called on to bless the youngest child of the branch president. The mother, however, was embittered, and refused to allow her dying child to receive the blessing. "Not wishing to intrude," Eli wrote, he and the branch president retired to an upper room in the house to pray for the baby's life. The angry, suspicious mother sent one of her older daughters to watch them. Elder Pierce then reported, "In a secluded chamber we knelt down and prayed earnestly and fervently until we felt that the child would live and knew that our prayers had been heard."

Turning around, they saw the girl standing in the doorway, staring fixedly, but not at them. She seemed focused on a certain point in the room. She said nothing until her father spoke to her. And then she asked, "Papa, who was that other man in there?"

Her father answered, "That is Brother Pierce. You know him."

"No, I mean that other man."

"There was no other, darling, except Brother Pierce and myself. We were praying for Baby."

The girl shook her head and said with perfect composure, "Oh yes, there was. I saw him standing between you and Mr. Pierce and he was all dressed in white."

Elder Pierce concluded, "The baby was speedily restored to perfect health."

"The Lord requireth the heart and a willing mind" (D&C 64:34), and when we give it to Him, oh, the good He will do.

Source

Biography and Family Record of Lorenzo Snow, 407–413.

Emily Hill

By Glenn Rawson

Writer, producer, and host of the *Joseph Smith Papers* and *History of the Saints* television series

Emily was born in England in 1836 and grew up with an unusual interest in God. "I was much concerned about my eternal salvation," she said, "and felt I would make any sacrifice to obtain it." She asked questions, but no one could help her. She found answers and comfort in the scriptures. The prophet who most fed her tender soul was Isaiah. "I was never weary of reading his prophecies," she said; "the glory of a Latter-day Zion that burdened his inspirations possessed for me a charm irresistible."

Then when Emily was twelve, a cousin invited her family to attend a meeting of the church she had just joined. No one in the family was willing to go. Then one of her sisters volunteered the willing Emily. "Yes, send Em. She will tell us all about it."

Emily went, and there witnessed the gifts and power of the Spirit poured out in a way she had never seen. She was converted. "It was indeed as though I had been brought out of darkness into marvelous light," she said, "and I could not shut my eyes against it."

However, when she returned home and announced her desire to be baptized, not only was that privilege denied but ever after she was "closely watched lest [she] should be led away by a sect that was everywhere spoken against."

This went on for four years. In time, her sister Julia found the faith. While Emily and Julia were able to be baptized, immigrating to Zion was out of the question. Meanwhile, Emily was given a blessing that someday she would write in prose and verse and thereby comfort the hearts of thousands.

In May 1856, Emily and Julia ran away to Zion aboard the ship Thornton. In July 1856, they became a part of the Willie handcart company. It was a hard journey, and Emily wondered how she would ever make it—yet somehow she determined that not only would she go on, but she would pull that loaded handcart a thousand miles and never ride a step.

On Sunday, October 19, 1856, about noon, howling winter storms caught the Willie handcart company on one of the most exposed portions of the trail. They were completely out of food and were still hundreds of miles from Salt Lake. Suddenly three men rode in announcing that rescue wagons and supplies were just a couple of days away.

As the three rescuers were preparing to ride on to the east in search of the Martin Company, one of them—Joseph A. Young—saw among the sufferers someone he knew: Emily Hill. He burst into tears.

"Why do you cry, Brother Young?" she asked.

"Oh, because you look so starved and the provision wagons are miles away." With that he gave her the only thing he could—an onion. Rather than eat it, Emily held on to it. That night she saw a man near the fire who appeared to be dying. Emily gave the onion to him. That onion saved his life.

Emily and Julia made it to the valley. In time they both married. Then, when Emily had a child, her husband unexpectedly went on a mission, leaving her to fend for herself. Four years later he wrote back announcing that he was not coming home. The man repudiated his faith and renounced his families.

Significantly, Emily said, "All that I had hitherto suffered seemed like child's play compared to being deserted by one in whom I had chosen to place the utmost confidence."

It was now the winter of 1863–1864. The Civil War had driven prices up. Survival was difficult. Emily's house was sold out from under her. One night when she was weary with overwork and anxiety, pondering what to do, words came into her mind so clear as if audibly spoken: "Trust in God and thyself."

Emily got up, penned her heart's feelings in poetry, and went to work. In time she would remarry, bear eight children, and by the things that she suffered would become gifted in business, cheerful in nature, a champion of women's rights, and one of Zion's great poets.

You may not know her full name—Emily Hill Mills Woodmansee—but you will surely recognize the words she paid such a price to write:

"As sisters in Zion, we'll all work together . . ."

C. S. Lewis once said, "It is a serious thing to live in a society of possible gods and goddesses, to remember that the dullest most uninteresting person you can talk to may one day be a creature which, if you saw it now, you would be strongly tempted to worship. . . . There are no ordinary people. You have never talked to a mere mortal." No matter our age and circumstance, we do not yet know what we are fully capable of when we give ourselves into the hands of Christ.

Sources

Andrew Olsen, *The Price We Paid: The Extraordinary Story of the Willie and Martin Handcart Pioneers* (Salt Lake City, Utah: Deseret Book, 2006).

C. S. Lewis, *The Weight of Glory* (New York: HarperOne, 2001).

First Miracle in the Church

By William G. Hartley
Retired professor of history, Brigham Young University

The Lord once promised, "And these signs shall follow them that believe; in my name shall they cast out devils" (Mark 16:17). The Lord did not limit that promise in time. It is as applicable in these days as in those.

After the meeting to organize the Church of Christ on April 6, 1830, in Fayette, New York, the Knight relatives returned to Colesville. Soon afterward, Joseph Smith "went [on a visit] to the residence of Mr. Joseph Knight's—of Colesville—Broom Co. N.Y with whom I had been formerly well acquainted, as well as with his family and in the Neighborhood generally." The Knight family, Joseph Smith said, were Universalists "but were as usual glad to see (me) and very friendly and willing to reason on the subject of religion."

In April, Joseph Smith held "several meetings in the neighborhood" that were well attended. "We had many friends and some enemies," he noted. "Many began to pray fervently to Almighty God to give them wisdom to understand the truth."

Newel Knight was among those who attended the meetings regularly. Joseph Smith said that he and Newel "had many and serious conversations on the important subject of man's eternal salvation." Members "had got in the habit of praying much at our meetings," Joseph Smith said, and he noticed that Newel, like Father Knight, hesitated to pray vocally. So the Prophet tried to help. He wrote:

> Newel promised me on a certain day, that he would that evening take up his cross and pray vocally in the meeting the same evening. The evening came and the meeting was held, but when Newel was asked to pray, he begged to be excused. I tried to prevail upon him, and encourage him to pray. He replied that when he got out in the woods by himself he should there take up his cross . . .

Newel retired to the woods, Joseph continued, "where according to his own account afterwards he made several attempts to pray, but could scarcely do so, feeling as he said, that he had not done his duty, but that he should have taken up his cross in the presence of others." Joseph's friend "began to feel uneasy and felt worse both in mind and body, until upon reaching his own house, his appearance was such as to alarm his wife very much." Newel sent Sally to bring Joseph Smith to him. She did.

Then, according to the young prophet,

> I went and found him suffering very much in his mind, and his body acted upon in a most strange manner. His visage and limbs distorted & twisted into every possible shape and appearance, and finally he was caught up off the floor of the apartment and tossed about most fearfully. His situation was soon made known to his neighbors

> and relatives and in a short time as many as eight or nine grown persons had got together to witness the scene. After he had thus suffered for some time, I succeeded in getting hold of him by the hand, when almost immediately he was able to speak, and requested with great earnestness that I should cast the devil out of him, that he knew that he was in him, and that he also knew that I could cast him out. I replied, "If you know that I can, it shall be done." And almost unconsciously I rebuked the Devil, and commanded him in the name of Jesus Christ to depart from him. When immediately, Newel spoke out and said that he saw the Devil leave him and vanish from his sight.

Many witnessed Newel's possession and "saw the Devil thus cast out, of a human being and the power of God and His Holy Spirit thus made manifest."

But then, almost immediately, Newel experienced another encounter with the spiritual world, this time not from the dark side, but from God. His spirit entered into a rapturous revelation. Joseph Smith said the scene then entirely changed. "As soon as the Devil had departed from this our friend his countenance became natural, his distortions of body ceased, and almost immediately the Spirit of God descended upon him, to such a degree that the visions of eternity were opened to his view and he beheld great and glorious things."

Not until later did Newel tell Joseph Smith what happened during that visionary experience. "He afterwards related his experience," Joseph Smith said by way of preface to his including it in his history right after his account of the miracle of casting out the devil. Joseph then quoted Newel's own account of what he experienced while overcome by the spirit:

> I now began to feel a most pleasing sensation resting upon me, and immediately the visions of heaven were opened to my view. I felt [myself] attracted [up]wards, and remained for some time enwrapt [in] contemplation insomuch that I knew not what was going on in the room, but by and by I felt some weight pressing upon my shoulder and the side of my head, which served to recall me to a sense of my situation—and I found that the Spirit of the Lord had actually lifted me off the floor, and that my shoulder & head were pressing against the beams.

Newel said that during the vision, he "saw heaven opened and beheld the Lord Jesus Christ seated at the right hand of the Majesty on High. And this is my testimony, it was not a dream but a vision like the vision of Stephen, who on the day of his martyrdom had a similar view."

When Newel regained consciousness he was physically weak, so his associates placed him on a bed and waited upon him for some time. Joseph would describe this as the first miracle in the Church.

Sources

The Papers of Joseph Smith, 1:246–247.
History of the Church, 1:81–83.

Five Secret Questions

By Matthew C. Godfrey
MANAGING HISTORIAN, *JOSEPH SMITH PAPERS*

NOTHING THAT WE ARE IS hidden from the Lord, as is beautifully illustrated in this story.

William E. McLellin is an enigmatic figure in the early history of the Church. Baptized in 1831 and ordained one of the original Twelve Apostles in 1835, he had a volatile association with Joseph Smith and the Church and was eventually excommunicated in 1838. After this severing of ties, McLellin still could not leave the Church alone, writing numerous letters and articles about why he believed Joseph Smith was a fallen prophet. In all of these diatribes against Joseph and the Church, however, McLellin could never speak against an experience he had soon after his 1831 conversion—one that provided him with concrete evidence that Joseph was a prophet of God.

In October 1831, McLellin attended a general conference of the Church in Orange, Ohio. There he met the Prophet Joseph and other Church leaders for the first time, his soul thrilling in these encounters. After the conference was over, McLellin accompanied Joseph back to Hiram, Ohio, where

Joseph was living at the John and Elsa Johnson home and working on his translation of the Bible.

While at the Johnson home, McLellin found a private place and prayed to the Lord that He would make known to the Prophet Joseph answers to five specific questions that McLellin had. These questions, McLellin later recalled, "had dwelt upon my mind with anxiety." Without telling Joseph of the five questions or of his pleas to God, McLellin petitioned the Prophet to reveal to him the Lord's will. Joseph then received what is now section 66 of the Doctrine and Covenants—a revelation directed to McLellin. That revelation, McLellin declared, completely answered his five questions and was irrefutable evidence to him of the Prophet's divine calling.

This experience made such an impression on McLellin that nearly seventeen years later—several years after his departure from the Church—he still regarded the revelation as something clearly from God. "I now testify in the fear of God, that every question which I had thus lodged in the ears of the Lord of Sabbaoth, were answered to my full and entire satisfaction," he declared in January 1848. "I desired it for a testimony of Joseph's inspiration," he continued, "and I to this day consider it to me an evidence which I cannot refute."

The Prophet Joseph had inquired of the Lord, and the Lord had spoken. Of that McLellin was sure.

Truly, "There is none else save God that knowest thy thoughts and the intents of thy heart" (D&C 6:16).

Sources

Revelation, 29 Oct. 1831 [D&C 66], in Matthew C. Godfrey, Mark Ashurst-McGee, Grant Underwood, Robert J. Woodford, and William G. Hartley, eds., *Documents, Volume 2: July 1831–January 1833*, vol. 2 of the Documents series of *The Joseph Smith Papers*, ed. Dean C. Jessee, Ronald K. Esplin, and Richard Lyman Bushman (Salt Lake City, Utah: Church Historian's Press, 2013), 87–92.

William E. McLellin, Editorial, *Ensign of Liberty*, January 1848, 60–62.

Matthew C. Godfrey, "William McLellin's Five Questions," *Revelations in Context*, https://history.lds.org/article/doctrine-and-covenants-william-mclellin?lang=eng.

"Get Thee Out of Thy Country": The Dreams of Leonora Cannon Taylor

By Mary Jane Woodger
PROFESSOR OF CHURCH HISTORY AND DOCTRINE,
BRIGHAM YOUNG UNIVERSITY

THE LORD ONCE SAID, "My thoughts are not your thoughts, neither are your ways my ways, saith the Lord" (Isaiah 55:8). His declaration was to be richly illustrated in the life of Leonora Cannon Taylor.

As a spinster, Leonora Cannon was asked by a Mr. Mason to accompany his wife on a voyage to Canada. It was recorded that "she could not think of such a thing, but upon being urged, she made it a matter of prayer." Whenever Leonora had to make decisions it was her habit to ask the Lord in prayer to direct her to find her answers in the Bible. As Leonora prayed, she randomly opened her Bible to the following verse given to Abraham: "Get thee out of thy country, and from thy kindred and from thy father's house, into a land that I will shew thee" (Genesis 12:1). After reading this verse she was convinced that "it was the will of God that she should make the voyage," and she consented to accompany Mrs. Mason to the New World. They left in May 1832.

Leonora's future husband, John Taylor had joined the Methodists in 1824. From that time on, John Taylor had a keen awareness of his future: he was to become a Methodist minister and preach the gospel in Canada. John and Leonora began to have gospel discussions, and "John confided in Leonora [a] revelation in his youth through which he knew he would preach the gospel in America, and it was a message of greater import and power than he then had."

Both John and Leonora were searching for the truth, but John found something else; he was falling in love with Leonora. On the other hand, Leonora was not interested in any kind of a relationship with John other than minister and parishioner. When John finally got up his nerve to propose marriage, she without any hesitancy rejected it. She had not been thinking about him romantically. One problem was an age difference—John Taylor was twenty-five and Leonora Cannon was thirty-seven.

Not wanting to accept Leonora's rejection, John turned to prayer, asking the Lord to soften Leonora's heart. Subsequently, Leonora had a vivid dream where she saw "herself associated with him [John Taylor] in his life-work, and from this spiritual manifestation she became convinced that John Taylor was to be her husband." She accepted this dream as revelation, and John and Leonora were "married in the Episcopal Church of Toronto on January 28, 1833, by Reverend Mr. Lockheart."

How could she have known in those beginning years that she would become the wife of a man every bit as much a prophet as those she revered in her Bible?

Sources

Mary Alice Cannon Lambert, "Leonora Cannon Taylor," *The Young Women's Journal*, 19:346.

Brigham H. Roberts, *Comprehensive History of The Church of Jesus Christ of Latter-day Saints* (Salt Lake City, Utah: Deseret News Press, 1930), 1:255.

Matthias F. Cowley, *Reminiscences of President John Taylor*, typescript of an address at L.D.S. University Breakfast Club, Oct. 4, 1925, Church History Department Archives.

Note in Taylor Family Bible in "President John Taylor and His Wives," *Our Pioneer Heritage*, vol. 7, 1964, 219.

"Get Up and Move That Carriage"

By Susan Easton Black

Emeritus professor of Church history and doctrine,
Brigham Young University

Wilford Woodruff wrote much about the Spirit of the Lord guiding and protecting him. For example, when he responded to Brigham Young's call to "gather every Saint of God in New England and Canada and send them up to Zion," Wilford penned:

> I drove my carriage one evening into the yard of Brother Williams. Brother Orson Hyde drove a wagon by the side of mine. I had my wife and children in the carriage. After I turned out my team and had my supper, I went to bed in the carriage. I had not been there but a few minutes when the Spirit said to me, "Get up and move that carriage." I told my wife I had to get up and move the carriage. She said, "What for?" I said, "I don't know." That is all she asked me on such occasions. When I told her I did not know, that was enough. I got up and

> moved my carriage. . . . I then looked around me and went to bed. The same Spirit said, "Go and move your animals from that oak tree." . . . I went and moved my horses and put them in a little hickory grove. I again went to bed.

Within "thirty minutes, a whirlwind came up and broke that oak tree off within two feet from the ground," wrote Wilford. "It swept over three or four fences and fell square in that dooryard, near Brother Orson Hyde's wagon, and right where mine had stood."

Wilford then asked himself, "What would have been the consequences if I had not listened to that Spirit? . . . That was the still, small voice to me—no earthquake, no thunder, no lightning; but the still, small voice of the Spirit of God."

Similarly, after gathering the New England Saints and bringing them down to Pittsburgh, Pennsylvania, Wilford penned,

> I saw a steamer just preparing to go out. I walked right up to the captain and asked him if he was ready to go out. He said he was.
>
> "How many passengers have you?"
>
> "Two hundred fifty."
>
> "Can you take another hundred?"
>
> "I can."
>
> "Then," said I, "I would like to go aboard with you."

As the words left his mouth, the Spirit of the Lord said to Wilford, "Don't you nor your company go aboard that steamer." For Wilford, there was no hesitation or rationalizing his need to quickly get the Saints to Zion. He wrote, "That was enough: I had learned the voice of the Spirit. I turned and told the captain that I had made up my mind not to go at present. That steamer started out. It was a dark night, and before the steamer had gone far she took fire, and all on board were lost. We should probably have shared the same fate had it not been for that monitor within me."

This is what the Lord meant when he said, "Behold, I will tell you in your mind and in your heart by the Holy Ghost which shall come upon you and which shall dwell in your heart" (D&C 8:2).

Sources

Deseret News Weekly, September 5, 1891.
Deseret News Weekly, November 7, 1896.

"God Is in This Storm"

By Mary Jane Woodger
Professor of Church history and doctrine,
Brigham Young University

When we are on the Lord's errand, He will fight our battles with us (see D&C 105:14). That promise was proven true through a remarkable experience of the Saints in Zion's Camp.

A company of about two hundred volunteers known as Zion's Camp left Kirtland on a rescue mission in May 1834 to help Church members "scattered on the land of Zion" (D&C 103:15). On June 18, Zion's Camp was forced to stop between the forks of the Big and Little Fishing Rivers. While they pitched their tents, five mob members rode into camp, swearing that the Mormons would "see hell before morning." When the camp heard sounds of gunfire and some of the men wanted to fight, the Prophet declared, "Stand still and see the salvation of God."

Within a few minutes a "small black cloud appeared in the clear western sky. It moved eastward, unrolling like a scroll, filling the heavens with darkness. As the first ferry load of mobbers crossed the Missouri River to the south, a sudden squall made it nearly impossible for the boat to return to pick up another load. The storm was so intense that Zion's Camp abandoned their tents and found shelter in an old Baptist meetinghouse nearby. When Joseph Smith came in, he exclaimed, "Boys, there is some meaning to this. God is in this storm."

The mob sought refuge, but found none as the storm broke tree limbs, scattered horses, and soaked ammunition, making it useless. It rained in torrents throughout the night. Thunder and lightning exceeded all description as small hailstones fell in Zion's Camp; outside Zion's Camp, the hailstones were the size of eggs. One of the mob was killed by lightning, and a horse, frightened by the stream that rose to a depth of thirty to forty feet, tore off the hand of a man who was trying to hold it.

The mob "declared that if that was the way God fought for the Mormons, they might as well go about their business."

A Colonel Sconce remarked, "There is an Almighty power that protects this people, for I started . . . having a fixed determination to destroy you, but was kept back by the storm."

A number of the men of Zion's Camp remembered that storm as the worst they had ever seen. With the numbers of the assembled mob and the comparative weakness of the camp, little but divine intervention could have kept the mob from destroying Zion's Camp.

Sources

George A. Smith, "Memoirs of George A. Smith," May 4, 1834, LDS Historical Department, Salt Lake City, Utah.

Milton V. Backman Jr., *The Heavens Resound, A History of the Latter-day Saints in Ohio 1830–38* (Salt Lake City, Utah: Deseret Book, 1983).

Joseph Holbrook History, 17, *Joseph Smith Papers*, http://josephsmithpapers.org/person?name=Joseph+Holbrook.

B. H. Roberts, *A Comprehensive History of the Church of Jesus Christ of Latter-day Saints* (Salt Lake City, Utah: Deseret News, 1957).

David F. Boone, "Zion's Camp: A Study in Obedience, Then and Now," in *Sperry Symposium Classics: The Doctrine and Covenants*, Craig K. Manscill, ed. (Provo, Utah: Religious Studies Center, Brigham Young University, 2004).

"Greatest Desire of My Heart"

By Glenn Rawson

WRITER, PRODUCER, AND HOST OF THE *JOSEPH SMITH PAPERS* AND *HISTORY OF THE SAINTS* TELEVISION SERIES

ALL OF US MATTER TO the Lord, no matter who or what we are—a principle beautifully illustrated in the story of a man named Orson.

When Orson was about eighteen years old, his soul was awakened unto God. He began to "pray very fervently, repenting of every sin. In the silent shades of night, while others were slumbering upon their pillows," he said, "I often retired to some secret place in the lonely fields or solitary wilderness, and bowed before the Lord and prayed for hours with a broken heart and contrite spirit; this was my comfort and delight. The greatest desire of my heart," he would reflect, "was for the Lord to manifest His will concerning me."

In time, two missionaries came into the area where he lived; one of them was his older brother. As they preached, Orson recognized the truth; on September 19, 1830, his nineteenth birthday, he was baptized—the only individual to be baptized in that area for many years afterward.

Orson immediately set out on a journey of 230 miles to the west, looking for the Prophet Joseph Smith. By November 4, 1830,

Orson found the Prophet at the home of Father Whitmer in Fayette, New York. Now, after so many years of searching for the Lord and wanting to know His will concerning him, Orson had found someone who could tell him.

When Orson asked Joseph, Joseph told him that it was his privilege to know. He invited Orson into the chamber of old Father Whitmer, and by the aid of the seer stone began to dictate the word and will of Almighty God for Orson Pratt. When he invited the humble lad to write it down, Orson declined, considering himself not worthy. Could John Whitmer do it? Yes! And John recorded the revelation we know today as section 34 of the Doctrine and Covenants.

In that revelation was given a promise that, to one of such humble origins as Orson, seemed almost too great to attain to. It was, "Lift up your voice and prophesy, and it shall be given by the power of the Holy Ghost." How could he ever live up to that?

Shortly afterward, Orson was ordained an elder and sent forth. Notwithstanding his weakness, Orson would become one of the most influential leaders of the Church in the nineteenth century.

He was always a missionary. He was the first one into the Salt Lake Valley in 1847. Among many other things, it was he who from 1876–1879 prepared new editions of the scriptures, adding revelations to the Doctrine and Covenants—such as Doctrine and Covenants 121–123—and dividing the Book of Mormon into chapters and verses.

On October 3, 1881, after fifty-one years of giving his life to the cause of Christ, Orson Pratt passed away.

The Master once said, and it is applicable here, "Are not two sparrows sold for a farthing? And one of them shall not fall on the ground without your Father. But the very hairs of your head are all numbered. Fear ye not therefore, ye are of more value than many sparrows" (Matthew 10:29–31). He knows us, and He loves us.

Sources

http://josephsmithpapers.org/paperSummary/revelation-book-1?p=29&highlight=Orson.

https://history.lds.org/article/doctrine-and-covenants-orson-pratt?lang=eng.

Healing of Philo Dibble

By William G. Hartley
Retired professor of history, Brigham Young University

The Apostle James commanded, "Is any sick among you? Let him call for the elders of the Church; and let them pray over him, anointing him with oil in the name of the Lord: and the prayer of faith shall save the sick, and the Lord shall raise him up" (James 5:14). This power and promise is still in effect, as the following story so richly illustrates.

In late 1833, certain local citizens in Jackson County, Missouri, had determined to drive the Mormons from the county by whatever means necessary. Hence, on November 4, 1833, a large band of Missourians captured the Mormon ferry on the Big Blue River. Riders scattered among the Saints to recruit help. In response, thirty armed men jogged toward the ferry.

At sunset, the thirty men reached Christian Whitmer's house, where mobbers were bullying him. Firing commenced. Joseph Knight Jr., working at his mill a mile away, could hear the shooting.

In the skirmish, two Missourians and several horses were killed. Andrew Barber, a Mormon, became "the first man in this dispensation who was martyred for the truth's sake," Newel Knight eulogized. Brother Philo Dibble was shot in the stomach. A veteran doctor examined him and declared the wounds to be fatal.

Eluding a mob near the house where Dibble lay, Newel slipped inside and went to the victim's bed. "I drew the bed curtains with one hand and laid the other upon his head, praying secretly" in his behalf, Newel said. Then he left immediately to avoid the mob.

The next day, business took Newel some ten miles from the place—where, to his surprise, Newel said "I met Bro. Dibble making his escape from the county":

> He told me that as soon as I placed my hand on his head the pain and soreness seemed gradually to move as before a power driving it, until in a few minutes it left his body. He then discharged about a gallon of putrid matter, and the balls and pieces of clothing which had passed into his body.

Philo Dibble wrote about this wonderful healing too, and his account adds details not in Newel's recounting:

> After the surgeon left me, Brother Newel Knight came to see me. He sat on the right side of my bed and laid his hand on my head but never spoke. I felt the spirit resting upon me at the crown of my head before his hand touched me and I knew immediately that I was going to be healed. It seemed to form like a ring under the skin and followed down my body. When the ring came to the wound, another ring formed around the first bullet hole, also the second and

> third. Then the ring formed on each shoulder and on each hip and followed down to my fingers and toes and left me. I immediately arose and discharged three quarts of blood or more, with some pieces of my clothes that had been driven into my body by the bullets. I then dressed myself and went out doors. . . . From that time not a drop of blood came from me and I never afterwards felt the slightest pain or inconvenience from my wound except that I was somewhat weak from the loss of blood.

Brother Dibble lived for many years after being shot. Of this event, Newel Knight recorded this in his diary: "O how our hearts rejoiced and gave thanks to that God who had heard and answered the secret prayer of his servant, although in the midst of an infuriated mob."

Sources

William G. Hartley, *Stand by My Servant Joseph: The Story of the Joseph Knight Family* (Joseph Fielding Smith Institute: 2003).

Philo Dibble's statement is in Clare B. Christensen, *Before and After Mt. Pisgah* (Salt Lake City, Utah: privately published, 1979), 79.

"I Have Taken Them to Myself"

By Glenn Rawson

STORYTELLER ON THE *SOUNDS OF SUNDAY* RADIO PROGRAM

ONE OF THE ROLES OF the Holy Ghost is to be a comforter. The events surrounding the martyrdom of Joseph and Hyrum Smith provide a definite example of that role.

On June 27, 1844, a mob stormed the jail in Carthage, Illinois, shouting and shooting, their hearts bent on murder. By the time it was over, two brothers who had been wrongfully imprisoned—Joseph and Hyrum Smith—were dead.

A short time later, the two martyred sons were taken home to Nauvoo. Thousands lined the road in mourning as they passed. They were taken to the Mansion House in Nauvoo, where friends prepared their bodies for viewing. A short time later the family, who had been grieving and awaiting their return, entered the room. Joseph's wife Emma attempted several times to cross the room to her husband, but each time she fainted. Finally, she was helped from the room. Mary Fielding came next. "She trembled at every step, and nearly fell, but reached her husband's body. . . . a gushing plaintive wail burst from her lips. . . . Her grief seemed to consume her and she lost all power of utterance."

It was then that the venerable and aged mother, Lucy Mack Smith, came into the room. "I had for a long time," she said, "braced every nerve, roused every energy of my soul, and called upon God to strengthen me, but when I entered the room and saw my murdered sons extended both at once before my eyes and heard the sobs and groans of my family . . . it was too much; I sank back, crying to the Lord in the agony of my soul, 'My God, my God, why hast thou forsaken this family!'"

"I have taken them to myself, that they might have rest," came a voice in reply.

As she stood between the bodies of her sons, resting a hand upon each one, looking down at their peaceful smiling countenances, she heard their voices in her mind: "Mother, weep not for us, we have overcome the world by love; we carried to them the gospel, that their souls might be saved; they slew us for our testimony, and thus placed us beyond their power; their ascendancy is for a moment, ours is an eternal triumph."

One month later, Lucy would lose another son, Samuel, to the mobs. She had borne eight sons and had reared six to manhood; now only one remained. If ever a woman could curse God and wish to die it was Mother Lucy. But she did not.

Near the end of her life, Enoch Tripp paid her a visit in Nauvoo. When Lucy learned he was from Salt Lake, she reached up from her bed, put her arms around his neck, and kissed him, declaring that she could now die in peace, having seen someone from the valley. She told him that she wanted to go west too but was prevented. She bade him give her love to Brigham, Heber, and all the other righteous Saints, for her heart was with them.

She passed away May 4, 1856, true and faithful to the end.

Sources

Lucy Mack Smith, *History of Joseph Smith by His Mother* (Salt Lake City, Utah: Deseret Book, 2009).

http://josephsmithpapers.org/paperSummary/lucy-mack-smith-history-1845?p=321&highlight=Braced%20every%20nerve.

"In Our Extremities"

By Susan Easton Black
Emeritus professor of Church history and doctrine,
Brigham Young University

On Saturday, October 4, 1856, Brigham Young was informed that two handcart companies were still en route to the Salt Lake Valley. The next day at the semiannual general conference, where nearly twelve thousand Saints had gathered, President Young said:

> Many of our brethren and sisters are on the plains with hand-carts, and probably many are now 700 miles from this place, and they must be brought here, we must send assistance to them. The text will be, to get them here. . . . Go and bring in those people now on the plains.

The response was immediate. Men saddled horses and loaded wagons with needed supplies for their journey of some three hundred miles to the windswept snow drifts of Wyoming. On October 7, the first of what would be two hundred and fifty rescue teams moved out from the Salt Lake Valley. On October 21, rescuers reached the Willie Company: "Shouts of joy rent the air; strong men wept till tears ran freely down their furrowed and sun-burnt cheeks." Some in the first rescue party stayed with the Willie Company, while others pushed on in search of the Martin Company.

"We found the Martin Company in a deplorable condition," wrote rescuer George D. Grant. "There were old men pulling and tugging their carts, sometimes loaded with a sick wife or children—women pulling along sick husbands—little children six to eight years old struggling through the mud and snow. . . . The sight is almost too much for the stoutest of us."

It was not until November 9 that the first members of the Willie Company entered the Salt Lake Valley. Twenty-one days later, on November 30, survivors of the Martin Company began their descent into the valley. President Young, speaking to a congregation in the bowery on Temple Square, said:

> I wish the sisters to go home and prepare to give those who have just arrived a mouthful of something to eat, and to wash them and nurse them up. You know that I would give more for a dish of pudding and milk, or a baked potato and salt, were I in the situation of those persons who have just come in, than I would for all your prayers, though you were to stay here all the afternoon and pray. Prayer is good, but when baked potatoes, and pudding, and milk are needed, prayer will not supply their place on this occasion.

Years later, when Francis Webster, a survivor of the Martin handcart company, heard critics speak disparagingly of the handcart movement, he said:

> You are discussing a matter you know nothing about. . . . I was in that Company and my wife was in it. . . . We suffered beyond anything you can imagine and many died of exposure and starvation, but did you ever hear a survivor of that Company utter a word of criticism? Not one of that Company ever apostatized or left the Church because every one of us came through with the absolute knowledge that God lives for we became acquainted with him in our extremities.

Sources

"Brigham Young Speech at the Bowery," *Deseret News*, October 15, 1856.

"Mr. Chislett's Narrative," in T. B. H. Stenhouse, *The Rocky Mountain Saints: A Full and Complete History of the Mormons from the First Vision of Joseph Smith to the Last Courtship of Brigham Young . . . and the Development of the General Mineral Wealth of the Territory of Utah* (New York: D. Appleton and Co., 1873), 325.

William R. Palmer, "Pioneers of Southern Utah," *Instructor*, May 1944, 217–218.

Isaac Leany's Miraculous Recovery

By Alexander L. Baugh

Professor of Church history and doctrine,
Brigham Young University

It is a question still worth asking that we might be reminded forcefully of the answer—"Is anything too hard for the Lord" (Genesis18:14)? And the answer is still no!

In the late afternoon of October 30, 1838, an anti-Mormon vigilante force consisting of more than two hundred armed men with blackened faces attacked the relatively defenseless Mormon settlement of Hawn's Mill located in eastern Caldwell County, Missouri. Seventeen Mormon men and boys were killed in the fray or died shortly afterward. Another fifteen were wounded, including one woman.

At the time of the attack, a number of Mormon men rushed into the village blacksmith shop, where they held off their attackers for several minutes, but the vigilante force eventually secured positions directly outside the walls of the shop. Seeing no other recourse, many of the Mormon defenders attempted to make a break from the building. One of those was Isaac Leany, who made a harrowing and miraculous escape.

When Isaac left the shop, he was pelted with bullets and hit several times. In spite of his injuries, he was able to make his way to the mill, where he climbed down one of the mill's timbers to the creek; then he waded through the frosty water until he came to Jacob Hawn's home, where several Mormon women attended to his wounds. Fearing the mob might storm the house and discover Isaac, the women removed a floorboard, laid him down in an open space under the floor, and resecured the board. Here he remained until the vigilantes left.

By late evening, Isaac Leany lay nearly lifeless and was not expected to live. An examination of his wounds showed that four balls had passed entirely through his body, leaving eight holes. He was also grazed by two more bullets, resulting in flesh wounds to each arm. Twenty-seven bullet holes were counted in his shirt and another seven in his pants. With little hope he would ever recuperate, he was given a priesthood blessing in which he was promised a speedy convalescence. Isaac bore testimony that upon being blessed, he had no pain whatsoever and within four weeks was completely healed.

On May 6, 1839, at a conference of the Church held near Quincy, Illinois, Wilford Woodruff recorded meeting Isaac Leany, who showed him his wounds. He wrote that Leany received all of his wounds "while he was running for his life & strange as it may appear all those wounds . . . did not lessen his speed in the least but he entirely out run his enemies & saved his life. We can only acknowledge it to be by the power & mercy of God."

Sources

Isaac Leany petitions in *Clark V. Johnson, Mormon Redress Petitions: Documents of the 1833–1838 Missouri Conflict* (Provo: Religious Studies Center, Brigham Young University, 1992), 267, 486.

John D. Lee, *Mormonism Unveiled* (St. Louis: Moffatt Publishing Co., 1881), 80–81.

Wilford Woodruff, *Wilford Woodruff's Journal, 1833–1898,* Scott G. Kenney, ed., 9 vols. (Midvale, Utah: Signature Books, 1983), 1:331.

"It Is of No Use"

By William G. Hartley

RETIRED PROFESSOR OF CHURCH HISTORY AND DOCTRINE,
BRIGHAM YOUNG UNIVERSITY

THE LORD SAID, "REQUIRE NOT miracles, except I shall command you, except casting out devils, healing the sick, and against poisonous serpents, and against deadly poisons; and these things ye shall not do, except it be required of you by them who desire it" (D&C 24:13–14). And when it is required of the Lord's authorized servants, wonderful things happen.

In 1843, the sailing ship Swanton carried 212 Latter-day Saints from Liverpool to New Orleans. It took two months at sea. As president of the company, Elder Lorenzo Snow wrote the following account of the voyage:

> We had been out to sea about two weeks during which nothing very material occurred more than what usually happens at sea, when the following occurrence transpired: The captain's steward, a young German, met with an accident which threatened his life. Being a very moral, sober, and steady young man, having

been with the Captain several voyages, he had succeeded greatly in winning the affections of the Captain, officers and crew. The Saints also had become much attached to him. Hence the prospects of his death so [created] a great sensation of sorrow and grief throughout the whole ship. He would bleed at his mouth [and was] attended with severe cramping and fits. At last, after having tried various remedies to no purpose, all hopes of his life were given up. The sailors before retiring to their beds were requested by the captain to go into the cabin one by one to bid him farewell; which accordingly was done without the least expectation of seeing him alive the next morning. Many eyes were wet with tears as they returned from the cabin. Sister [Ann] Martin from Bedford while sitting alone by his bedside expressed to him her wish that I might be called on and administer to him, and perhaps he might yet be restored. To this he gave a cheerful consent.

I was asleep in my berth when the message came, it being about twelve o'clock of the night. I arose immediately and proceeded to the cabin. On the way [I] met the first mate who had just been to see him. As soon as he passed me, he met Brother Staines and observed to him that Mr. Snow was going in to lay hands on the steward, but says he (in a sorrowful strain) it is all of no use, it is all over with the poor fellow now. "Oh," says Elder Staines, "the Lord can restore him through the laying on of hands." "Good God!! Do you think so?" [returned] the sailor in the simplicity of his heart.

As I passed along, I met the captain at the cabin door who appeared to have been weeping. "I am glad you have come Mr. Snow," said he, "tho it is of no use for it must soon be over with the Steward." I stepped into his room and sat down by his bed. His breathing was very short and seemed as one dying. He could not speak loud, but signified his wish I should administer to him. It appeared he had a wife and two children in Hamburg, Germany who were dependent upon him for their support. He seemed much troubled about them.

I laid my hands upon his head, and had no sooner got through the administration than he arose up into a sitting posture spotted his hands together shouting praises to the Lord for being healed. Very soon after he arose from his bed went out of the cabin and walked the deck. The next morning everybody was astonished to see the steward alive, and amazed to see him able to go about his business as usual. The sailors, one and all, swore that was a miracle. The Saints know it to be so, [and] rejoiced and praised the Lord. The captain believed it firmly and felt deeply grateful, and his heart became knit with ours from that time forward. He granted us every favor and indulgence that was in his power to bestow, and constantly studied our convenience; attended all of our meetings, and bought and read our books. The mates also [did] the same, and when I left them at New Orleans [they] made me a promise that they would be baptized. I received a letter about a year afterwards from the chief mate who informed me they had both fulfilled their promise. The captain also declared his intention of receiving the gospel at some future time and [living] with the Saints. The steward was baptized when we reached New Orleans, and on parting with him made me a present of a Bible which I now keep.

Sources

Lorenzo Snow, *Journal and Letterbook*, 1836–1845 (LDS Church Archives, Ms 1330 1,) 65–92.

http://mormonmigration.lib.byu.edu/Search/showDetails/db:MM_MII/t:account/id:1177/keywords:sarah+coleman.

James and Elizabeth Bleak: A Legacy of Sacrifice and Service

By Andrew D. Olsen

AUTHOR OF *THE PRICE WE PAID: THE EXTRAORDINARY STORY OF THE WILLIE AND MARTIN HANDCART COMPANIES*

"FOR SOME DAYS PAST I have been asking the Lord to open my way to go . . . to Zion," James Bleak wrote in his diary in February 1855. "This day I received a promise that I should be supplied with the means, for which I feel very grateful." Twenty-five-year-old James Bleak (pronounced Blake) was president of the Church's Whitechapel Branch in London. He and his wife, Elizabeth, had been yearning to gather with the Saints in Salt Lake City since their baptism four years earlier.

By late 1855, James and Elizabeth had accumulated enough funds to make the journey. James sent the money to the mission office in Liverpool with instructions for emigration leaders in the United States to purchase a wagon and a team of oxen to carry his family across the plains.

At about this time, President Brigham Young announced the handcart plan, by which emigrants could make the overland journey for one-tenth of the cost of a wagon outfit. Church leaders encouraged those who could afford wagons to make a substantial sacrifice: forgo the wagon, use handcarts instead, and let the savings help others emigrate.

James anguished over this counsel. Elizabeth wasn't used to traveling, and their four children "were of tender years, ranging from six years . . . to eleven months." James had already endured staggering losses in his family. Four of his five siblings had died as infants, he had been orphaned as a teenager, and his only other sibling had died when James was eighteen. Traveling by handcart might increase the risk of more loss. Out of consideration for his wife and children, James decided to keep the wagon.

He changed his mind, however, when members of his branch decided to emigrate in the same way that he was—by wagon rather than handcart. "[I] had always striven to set a becoming example," James said, so he wrote to the mission president "asking to be numbered on the handcart list" and requesting that the excess funds be "used for emigration purposes." Subsequently, other members of his branch gave up their wagons for handcarts.

After arriving in America, the Bleak family became part of the Martin handcart company. During the four-month, thirteen-hundred-mile journey from Iowa City to Salt Lake City, they felt most keenly the sacrifice of their wagon. Partway across Nebraska, James became so weak and sick that others pulled him in their handcarts for twenty-one miles.

Even greater trials came the next month, when winter arrived and the Martin Saints began forty-two days in relentless snow, cold, and wind. One night, James and Elizabeth's five-year-old son, Thomas, appeared to have died. Writing about this experience years later, James recalled:

> [I] began by anointing him with consecrated oil, and praying over him. . . . Not a heartbeat or other sign of life was in the child, [so I] continued to

> administer, to chafe the limbs and body, and to call upon the Lord. . . . Finally, by God's power and blessing, the dear child unclosed his eyes and is now a resident of Salt Lake City, father of nine children and likewise a grandfather.

More than sixty members of the Martin company died during the first two weeks of winter storms. When the weather became even more severe, the five hundred remaining members sought shelter in a ravine that is now known as Martin's Cove. The ravine provided some protection from the elements, but the wind whipped down tents, and the temperature plunged to eleven degrees below zero. Because the food supply was dwindling, the people received only one-fourth of their normal daily rations—hardly enough to sustain life in such piercing cold. And yet on the second day, when his family was given only one pound of flour for all six of them, James Bleak wrote these remarkable words: "Through the blessing of our Father we felt as contented as when we had 1 lb per head."

After the Martin Saints had been in the cove for five days, the weather moderated enough for them to resume traveling the final 325 miles to Salt Lake City. By then, most of the people could no longer walk. Members of two wagon companies had unloaded wagons to carry them, but there wasn't enough room for everyone, and James didn't want to "burden the teams," so he hobbled five miles on frozen feet. "I have suffered very much today with my feet, which are frost-bitten," he wrote in his diary. The next day he rode in a wagon.

Despite their difficulties, James and Elizabeth Bleak and their four children all survived the journey. James's feet were so badly frozen that the flesh dropped off his heels and he wouldn't be able to walk for months. Nevertheless, he recorded this expression of faith and gratitude when he arrived in Salt

Lake City, Utah: "I feel to rejoice greatly and give praise to God for my safe arrival in Zion with my wife and children."

Five years later, in 1861, the Bleaks were among the first families called to settle St. George. James served as clerk and historian of the Southern Utah Mission for nearly fifty years. He also served in many civic capacities and in many other Church callings, including a mission to England at the age of forty-two.

When the St. George Temple was completed in 1877, James Bleak made it the focus of his life. He was the temple recorder for more than twenty years and worked closely with Wilford Woodruff, who was the temple president, and later served as the assistant president. Elizabeth was likewise a dedicated temple worker.

Elizabeth died in 1899, and James died in 1918 at age eighty-eight. At the time of his death, this man—who was the sole survivor of his family when he was just eighteen years old—had approximately 250 descendants.

Sources

James Bleak diary, Feb. 24, 1855, Church History Library.
Andrew Olsen, *The Price We Paid: The Extraordinary Story of the Willie and Martin Handcart Pioneers.*

Jedediah Morgan Grant

By Glenn Rawson

STORYTELLER ON THE *SOUNDS OF SUNDAY* RADIO PROGRAM

PRESIDENT HOWARD W. HUNTER ONCE said, "Please remember this one thing. If our lives and our faith are centered upon Jesus Christ and his restored Gospel, nothing can ever go permanently wrong. On the other hand, if our lives are not centered on the Savior and his teachings, no other success can ever be permanently right."

On September 2, 1847, on the Sweetwater River in Wyoming, Margaret Grant, the infant daughter of Jedediah and Caroline Grant, succumbed to cholera. She was buried on the side of a rolling clay hill not far from the trail. Her mother "[wept] as if her heart would break." Yet, notwithstanding the grief, the wagon train hitched up and moved on.

With the loss of her baby, Caroline Grant grew weaker and weaker. Then, on Sunday, September 26, 1847, somewhere south of present-day Evanston, Wyoming, Caroline slipped into critical condition. For the first time, there was no Sabbath singing or preaching heard in the camp; instead, the day was passed in fasting and prayer for Caroline's recovery. Around midnight, Caroline closed her eyes and seemed to be sinking.

To her husband, Jedediah, she whispered, "All is well! All is well! Please take me to the Valley—Jeddy. Get Margaret—bring her to me!"

"Brother Grant answered tenderly . . . as he sobbed with sorrow, 'Yes, yes, Caroline. I'll do my best. I'll do my best.'"

The next morning Jedediah Grant, true to his promise, set out for Salt Lake City with his beloved Caroline. Two days later he would lay her to rest in the valley. The entire community grieved at his loss. Caroline Grant was only twenty-nine years old and the first white woman buried in the Salt Lake Valley.

Days later, Jedediah and a friend, Joseph Bates Noble, sat close to a small fire under the night sky of Wyoming. Jedediah requested that they sing some hymns. When they finished, Jedediah "sat with bowed head for some time, then he looked up and, glowing with his former inspiration . . . declared in a firm voice . . . 'Bates, God has made it plain. The joy of paradise where my wife and baby are together, seems to be upon me tonight. For some wise purpose they have been released from the earth struggles into which you and I are plunged. They are many, many times happier than we can possibly be here.'"

Days later Jedediah and Bates reached the place where Margaret was buried. Bates described the events:

> A few paces from the little grave we stopped hesitatingly . . . and stood with eyes fixed before us. Neither tried to speak. An ugly hole replaced the small mound; and so recently had the wolves departed that every sign was fresh before us. I dared not raise my eyes to look at Jedediah. From the way I felt, I could but guess his feelings. Like statues of the wilderness we stood grown to the spot, each fully realizing that nothing more could be done. After several minutes of silent tears, we quietly withdrew,

> carrying away again only that which we had brought.

Nine years later, in November 1856, Jedediah Grant—now grievously ill himself—was granted a vision. He saw the world of spirits into which all will one day enter. He described the paradise of God as a heavenly place—beautiful beyond all description, filled with gardens, flowers, and buildings more glorious than anything found in this sphere. It was a place of perfect order, light, and cleanliness—a place of peace. Caroline came to him speaking words of comfort and instruction. She was beautiful. Margaret too was there, both glorious witnesses that the terrible tragedy of the plains was and would be overcome in the paradise of God.

On the night of December 1, 1856, Jedediah M. Grant passed into the world of spirits. Death can be cruel and unfair, but for the faithful it will be made right on the other side. All is well!

Sources

"Fear Not, Little Flock," *1988–89 Devotional and Fireside Speeches* (Provo, Utah: Brigham Young University Press, 1989), 112.

http://journal.segullah.org/summer-2007/and-should-we-die%E2%80%94all-is-well-doctrines-to-comfort-grieving-parents-on-the-mormon-trail/.

https://speeches.byu.edu/talks/brent-l-top_still-takes-faith/.

Joseph Millett

By Steven Olsen

Senior curator for historic sites for
The Church of Jesus Christ of Latter-day Saints

Joseph Millett was born in late December 1832 or 1833 in Earnest Town, Upper Canada (now Ontario), the eldest child of Artemus Millett and Susannah Peters. Susannah was Artemus's second wife; his first wife had died in 1831, leaving him with six children. Susannah died in 1841 after bearing four sons. Shortly after Susannah's death, Artemus and six living children (all sons), including Joseph, moved to Nauvoo, where they experienced many joys but much persecution. Five years later, they headed west with the Saints, arriving in Salt Lake City in 1850.

After two years' working with different groups of pioneers in central and southern Utah, Joseph accepted a call to serve a mission to Nova Scotia. Prior to leaving, he was endowed in the Endowment House on August 30, 1852, and was blessed on September 5 by his father and patriarch Isaac Morley. Five days later, he was blessed by Apostle Jedediah M. Grant.

Joseph traveled for seven months to reach his mission field, working his way across the continent and staying with family and friends along the way. He later reflected, "Many a time, I would turn in to the woods and brush, in some desolate place, with a full heart, wet eyes and face to call on my master for strength and aid. I believed the gospel of Christ. I never had preached it. I knew not where to find it in the scriptures. I had to give my bible to the boatman . . . for fare across."

During his mission, he traveled hundreds of miles throughout Nova Scotia, mostly without a companion, holding sacrament and prayer meetings, teaching the gospel, baptizing several, and experiencing miracles and other manifestations of divine watchcare. He frequently worked for his living and benefited from the generosity of residents, whether Latter-day Saint or not, for room, board, clothing, and other necessities. After nearly four years of full-time missionary service, Brother Millett returned home to Utah in the company of his wife, Sarah Elizabeth Glines, whom he had married on March 26, 1854, with the permission of his mission president, Elder Orson Pratt of the Quorum of the Twelve.

Between 1855 and 1872, ten children were born to Joseph and Sarah, some of whom died in childhood. During this time, the Millett family lived in a variety of communities in central and southern Utah and southern Nevada. Joseph supported the family financially through a number of occupations, including as a farmer, rancher, contractor, artisan, salesman, teamster, miner, and day laborer. In 1871, when the following event occurred, Joseph was selling and delivering produce and other goods to the residents of Pioche and the surrounding Nevada communities. He wrote:

> In 1871 one of my children came in, said that Brother Newton Hall's folks was out of bread, had none that day. I put our flour in sack to send to Brother Hall's. Just then Brother Hall came in. Ses I, "Bro. Hall, how are you out for flour?" "Brother Millett, we have none." "Well,

> Brother Hall, there is some in that sack. I have divided and was going to send it to you. Your children told mine that you was out." Brother Hall began to cry, said he had tried others, could not get any. Went to the cedars and prayed to the Lord, and the Lord told him to go to Joseph Millett. "Well, Brother Hall, you needn't bring this back if the Lord sent you for it. You don't owe me for it." You can't tell how good it made me feel to know that the Lord knew that there was such a person as Joseph Millett.

I wonder if the next time the Lord needs an angel of mercy in your neighborhood, could He send them to you?

There is a last part to this story that is seldom told—a "rest of the story," if you will. On July 26, 1901, in Washington, Utah, Joseph Millett had a dream in which he found himself at his own funeral. It disturbed him much that there were very few people present at the services, but then he looked again and saw a multitude of persons. He heard one say, "He baptized me with six others in Gaberouse Bay on the Island of Cape Breton." Another said, "He brought the Gospel to us on the Musquadobed in Nova Scotia." Still another said, "He baptized me and seven others in the Merrimac River at Lowell, Massachusetts." And on it went, people lauding the deeds of Joseph Millett. Newton Hall was there and spoke of that day in 1871 when he had been directed to obtain flour from Joseph Millet. And then one spoke and said, "I know him and shall speak for him." It was President Brigham Young.

Brother Millett realized that while there were few in mortal attendance at his funeral there were a multitude in attendance beyond the veil, praising and remembering the deeds of his life. These people were not mourning, but rejoicing, as was Brother Millett.

Joseph Millett passed away October 11, 1911, in Cedar City, Utah, having lived a life of charity. This is what the Lord meant when He commanded, "Stand in the office which I have appointed unto you; succor the weak, lift up the hands which hang down, and strengthen the feeble knees" (D&C 81:5). Thank the Lord for such individuals among us today.

Sources

Diary of Joseph Millett, Sr., photocopy of original, Church History Library, Salt Lake City, Utah.

Autobiography of Joseph Millett, photocopy of original, Church History Library, Salt Lake City, Utah.

Diary of Joseph Millett, holograph, Archives of The Church of Jesus Christ of Latter-day Saints, Salt Lake City, Utah.

https://familysearch.org/photos/stories/6943469.

Joseph J. Daynes

By Glenn Rawson

STORYTELLER ON THE *SOUNDS OF SUNDAY* RADIO PROGRAM

THE SCRIPTURES SPEAK OF TALENTS. It is a word with layers of meaning. In the Bible it denoted a unit of value and became the origin for our word for gifts and skills. The following is an example of what happens when foreordained talents are used in the Lord's service.

Joseph Daynes was born in England in 1851. His father was a watchmaker by trade but a musician by hobby. When Joseph was only eighteen months old, he showed a love of music. By the age of four he was performing, and at age six he was in demand for concerts and special performances. It is said he even performed for the Queen of England.

Then, in 1862, the family made the decision to immigrate to America. Joseph was only eleven years old and small of stature. As he walked across the trail going west, he carried a small harmonium strapped to his shoulders. In the evenings, alongside the trail, Joseph's father, John, would lead the singing while Joseph accompanied the weary travelers. This continued until the family arrived in Salt Lake City in June 1862. The company camped that first night on the old Pioneer Square, where the city/county building now stands—and as usual they sang while Joseph played.

In the audience that night, listening to young Joseph play was President Brigham Young. He had come to welcome them into the valley. He was heard to exclaim, "There is our organist for the great Tabernacle organ."

In 1866, President Young asked Joseph Ridges if he could build an organ for the new Tabernacle that was being constructed on Temple Square in Salt Lake City. Ridges said it could be done, and work was begun. All the while the organ was being built, people asked President Young, "Who will play our great organ when it is done?"

President Young would answer, "The Lord will provide."

On October 6, 1867, that organ was heard for the first time accompanying the Mormon Tabernacle Choir. Sitting at the console, only sixteen years old, was Joseph J. Daynes. He had to have a block of cork strapped to his feet to reach the pedals.

Joseph would hold that post as Tabernacle organist for the duration of the nineteenth century—thirty-three years. From that lad would come so many of the great hymns cherished around the world.

Mormon Tabernacle Choir conductor Evan Stephens later said of him, "He was, without doubt, one of the greatest organists of his time."

Source

http://www.daynesmusic.com/about/joseph-john-daynes.

Joseph's Vision

By Glenn Rawson

WRITER, PRODUCER, AND HOST OF THE *JOSEPH SMITH PAPERS* AND *HISTORY OF THE SAINTS* TELEVISION SERIES

LIKE THE STORY OF THE Creation itself, a sacred story has layers of detail that can be added or subtracted, veiled or revealed, depending on when it is told, who is telling it, and to whom the story is told. So it is with this story.

The year was 1818. Joseph Smith was about twelve years of age when he became "seriously impressed with the all-important concerns for the immortal soul." He "felt to mourn for [his] own sins" and "cried unto the Lord for mercy; considering it of first importance that [he] should be right in matters that involve eternal consequence." He attended the "several meetings" of the churches in his area, "as often as occasion would permit." He wanted to know which Church was true.

"I knew not who was right," he said. "I found that there was a great clash in religious sentiment; if I went to one society they referred me to one plan, and another to another, each one pointing to his own particular creed as the *summum bonum* of perfection."

In the midst of this war of words and tumult of opinions, Joseph often said to himself, "What is to be done? Who of all these parties are right . . . and how shall I know it?"

These questions led him to "searching the scriptures, believing . . . that they contained the word of God." One day he read in the Book of James, "If any of you lack wisdom, let him ask of God that giveth to all men liberally and upbraideth not and it shall be given him" (James 1:5).

"Never" he said, "did any passage of scripture come with more power to the heart of man than this did at this time to mine. . . . At length I came to the conclusion that I must either remain in darkness and confusion or else I must do as James directs."

Joseph "determined that [he] would ask [God]. I immediately went out into the woods," he said, "where my father had a clearing, and went to the stump where I had struck my axe. . . . I kneeled down and prayed."

No sooner had he done so than he was seized upon by some unseen power that completely overcame him. His mind was filled with darkness, doubt, and all manner of evil. The force was not an "imaginary ruin but . . . some actual being from the unseen world" that nearly killed him. Joseph exerted all his powers to call upon God, and then discovered a light exactly over his head brighter than the sun at noonday. He called it "a pillar of fire." The light descended gradually and "increased in brightness and magnitude, so that, by the time that it reached the tops of the trees, the whole wilderness, for some distance around was illuminated in a most glorious and brilliant manner."

The light "produced a peculiar sensation throughout [his] whole system." Joseph was "filled with the Spirit of God." He "saw two personages," he recorded, first one then the other, "whose brightness and glory defy all description, standing above me in the air." They "exactly resembled each other in features and likeness."

"One of them spake unto me," he said, "calling me by name and said, pointing to the other, 'This is my beloved son. Hear him.'"

Joseph later described that the personage was of a "light complexion, blue eyes, [with] a piece of white cloth drawn over his shoulders."

"Joseph, my son," the Lord said, "Thy sins are forgiven thee. Go thy way. Walk in my statutes and keep my commandments."

Joseph recorded, "No sooner did I get possession of myself so as to be able to speak, than I asked the personage who stood above me in the light, which of all the sects was right. I was answered that I must join none of them. I was expressly commanded 'to go not after them' at the same time receiving a promise that the fullness of the Gospel should at some future time be made known unto me." Joseph saw "many angels in this vision," and was told "many other things" that he did not write.

"For many days Joseph rejoiced with great joy for the Lord was with him." His soul was "filled with love," but then he added, "But [I] could find none that would believe the heavenly vision."

And thus is the story of one of the greatest visions in all of recorded history according to the several accounts left on record. For perspective, President Gordon B. Hinckley said of this vision,

> This is the pivotal thing of our story. Every claim we make concerning divine authority, every truth that we offer concerning the validity of this work, all find their roots in this First Vision of the boy prophet. . . . [It] becomes the hinge-pin on which this whole cause turns. If the First Vision was true, if it actually happened, then the Book of Mormon is true. Then we have the Priesthood. Then we have the Church organization and all of the other keys and blessings of authority which we say we have. Now it is

> just that simple. Everything turns on the reality of that First Vision. (Missionary meeting in Rochester, New York, July 12, 1996)

Sources

http://josephsmithpapers.org/site/accounts-of-the-first-vision?p=1&highlight=First%20Vision.

Church News, Feb. 1, 1997.

Joseph Toronto
and the Nauvoo Temple Gold

By Mary Jane Woodger
Professor of Church history and doctrine,
Brigham Young University

The Lord said, "All among them who know their hearts are honest, and are broken, and their spirits contrite, and are willing to observe their covenants by sacrifice—yea, every sacrifice which I the Lord, shall command—they are accepted of me" (D&C 97:9). The following is an example of a man who made just such a sacrifice.

As a youth, Joseph Toronto joined the Mediterranean Merchant Service in Italy and saved his wages. Once he had enough money, Joseph decided to try his luck in America. As he was sailing toward New York one night, he became very fearful that someone might steal his money. That night, "he had a dream in which a man stood before him, and told him to leave his money with 'Mormon Brigham' and he should be blessed." When he arrived in New York he asked everyone he met if they knew about "Mormon Brigham," but no one seemed to know him.

It was during a stay in Boston that Joseph first heard the Mormon missionaries preaching the gospel. When he heard the truth, he embraced it and was baptized. The missionaries then counseled Joseph to join with the Church in Nauvoo as soon as possible, but because he was doing so well financially, he refused to go at that time.

By the time Joseph Toronto finally immigrated to Nauvoo, Joseph Smith had been martyred and the Nauvoo Temple was being constructed. It was just a story high. Both persecution and the Saints' lack of finances made progress difficult. When the situation became critical on July 6, 1845, "Brigham Young announced that work on the temple would have to cease."

When Joseph heard President Young's announcement, he was deeply moved. The next afternoon, President Young recorded, "Joseph Toronto handed to me $2,500 in gold and said he wanted to give himself and all he had to the up-building of the church and kingdom of God."

Remembering the dream, Joseph Toronto donated his hard-to-come-by life savings to the building of the Nauvoo Temple. In turn, just as his dream had promised, President Young blessed Joseph that "he should stand at the head of his race and neither he nor his family should ever want for bread."

Sources

James A. Toronto, "Giuseppe Efisio Taranto: Odyssey from Sicily to Salt Lake City," in *Pioneers in Every Land*, Bruce A. Van Orden, D. Brent Smith, and Everett Smith Jr., eds. (Salt Lake City, Utah: Bookcraft, 1997), 126–127.

John R. Young, *Memoirs of John R. Young* (Salt Lake City, Utah: Deseret News, 1920), 47.

Alan F. Toronto, Maria T. Moody, and James A. Toronto, comp., *Joseph Toronto (Giuseppe Efisio Taranto)* (The Toronto Family Organization: June 25, 1983), 7.

Samuel W. Taylor, *Nightfall at Nauvoo* (New York: Avon Books, 1871), 356.

"Let Your Son Go"

By Susan Easton Black

Emeritus professor of Church history and doctrine,
Brigham Young University

"We were on our way to the mountains when the United States Officers came to our camp and told us their business," Drusilla Hendricks recalled. Their business was to get recruits to fight in the Army of the West in the Mexican War. As Drusilla thought upon the matter, she did not want her son William—the only eligible member of her family—to join the Mormon Battalion of the Army of the West. She reasoned, "My son was all I had to depend on, his father being helpless [an invalid] and Joseph my other son being in his ninth year only and my girls not very healthy."

Yet when Drusilla was alone, "whisperings of the spirit" seemed to say that William should join the battalion. "Are you afraid to trust the God of Israel? Has he not been with you in all your trials? Has he not provided for your wants?" she heard. She also heard a voice ask if she "did not want the greatest glory." Drusilla answered that she did. "Then how can you get it without making the greatest sacrifice?" asked the voice.

When Drusilla inquired, "Lord, what lack I yet?" the voice was heard to say, "Let your son go in the battalion." Believing these words were from God, Drusilla encouraged William to join the battalion on its epic march.

"I could not swallow one bit of breakfast," she later recollected, "but I waited on the rest thinking I might never have my family all together again. I had no photograph of him, but I took one in my mind and said to myself if I never see you again till the morning of the resurrection, I shall know you are my child. . . . I knelt down and told the Lord if he wanted my child to take him, only spare his life, and let him be restored to me and to the bosom of the Church. I felt it was all I could do. Then the voice that talked with me in the morning answered me saying, 'It shall be done unto you as it was unto Abraham when he offered Isaac on the Altar.'"

Believing these words were from the Lord, Drusilla ran to find William and said, "My son I have held you back but if you want to go [with the Mormon Battalion] I shall hold you no longer." Just over an hour later, William was gone.

In regard to the law of sacrifice, Elder M. Russell Ballard said, "If it becomes too easy to be a member of this Church, testimonies will become shallow, the roots of testimony will not go down into the soil like they did with our pioneer forefathers" ("The Law of Sacrifice," address to CES educators, Brigham Young University, Aug. 13, 1996). Drusilla Hendricks and her son were two of those pioneer forefathers who set the bar for us when it comes to sacrifice.

Source

Drusilla Dorris Hendricks, Oral History, "Historical Sketch of James Hendricks and Drusilla Dorris Hendricks (His Wife)," typescript, copied by James Roskelley from the original work, February 1904, L. Tom Perry Special Collections, Harold B. Lee Library, Brigham Young University, Provo, Utah, 38–41.

"Like Brass over My Head"

By Glenn Rawson

STORYTELLER ON THE *SOUNDS OF SUNDAY* RADIO PROGRAM

IN THE PARABLE OF THE importunate widow (see D&C 101:81–84), the Lord taught us to be persistent in prayer, even—and especially—when we don't want to. This story demonstrates why.

Years ago, there was a young college student who struggled with his testimony. Through the powerful influence of others, his heart was touched and he was convinced of the truthfulness of the gospel. I say "convinced," not converted. He did not yet know for himself by the witness of the Spirit that it was true. But acting on faith, he went forward and was baptized. For many days after that, he prayed, he studied, and he yearned, but still no witness as the Savior promised in the Gospel of John.

Late one afternoon while busily engaged in his studies, he became discouraged that he had not yet received an answer to his many prayers. The mood he was in became so oppressive that he couldn't study—couldn't even concentrate. So he went outside and wandered through the forests and fields near his home. The gloom of his mood however, only darkened.

Finally, he realized that it was time for prayer.

He had started a habit of going outside at a certain time and place each day for private prayer. But on this day and with this mood, he just did not feel like going to his grove to pray. "The heavens," he said, "seemed like brass over my head." One voice inside whispered that he should pray; the other voice enticed him away from his prayers.

Finally, after some struggle—or wrestle, if you will—he decided that he would keep his appointment with Heavenly Father. He knelt down, but no sooner had he opened his mouth than he heard something that resembled the rustling of silken robes over his head. The Spirit of God descended upon him from head to foot, filling him with an indescribable witness and joy. All darkness and doubt were gone in an instant, and he knew that Jesus Christ was the Son of God, and that the gospel was true. "I knew," he later said, "that God had conferred on me that which is of greater value than all the wealth and honors worlds can bestow."

From that day to the day of his death, he was true and gave his life to the witness he had gained. And what a life it was—the obedience, the sacrifices, the miracles. Lorenzo Snow was that young college student. He became a mighty man of God, and all because of a day when he prayed because he was supposed to, not because he wanted to.

Sources

Teachings of the Presidents of the Church: Lorenzo Snow (Salt Lake City, Utah: The Church of Jesus Christ of Latter-day Saints, 2012), 59–62.

https://books.google.com/books?id=TbuNO4UfMIkC&pg=PA127&lpg=PA127&dq=%22rustling+of+silken+robes%22&source=bl&ots=TbyzrLMUd4&sig=cPhLqJZinK_qJRquaTbG9h5nfIM&hl=en&sa=X&ei=JMloVcLFLoGfsQWU7IJI&ved=0CDsQ6AEwCQ#v=onepage&q=%22rustling%20of%20silken%20robes%22&f=false.

Luck of a Norwegian

By Max and Julie Parkin

Max Parkin is retired from the Church Educational System;
Julie Parkin teaches high school English

What would it have been like to sit at the feet of the Prophet Joseph Smith and listen to him speak?

Goudy Hogan was a teenager like any other—a little world-weary perhaps, but his life's experiences had matured him. Young Goudy was only eight years old when he and his family sailed from his home in Telemarken, Norway, to flee religious intolerance. Their dream was to own more land than the family's small farm in Norway.

Goudy survived that sea voyage to America that claimed some, including his three-year-old sister, Halja.

When the family arrived in America in 1837 and eventually settled in Ottawa, LaSalle County, where other Norwegians had settled in northern Illinois, Goudy was ready to be a kid again.

No such luck.

Once in the Chicago area, the family was traveling across a small body of water when their boat capsized and a portion of their luggage was lost—including $200, a small fortune in those days. A short time later, Goudy suffered the loss of another young sister, Marget.

At the tender age of nine, Goudy was hired out to move a man's livestock across the prairie. When his father came three months later to take Goudy home, he was distressed to see the worn condition of his young son, but Goudy only remembers the joy he felt at returning to his family.

Then, in 1842, after four years at Ottawa, the Hogan family was uprooted again when they moved to Sugar Creek, Lee County, Iowa, ten miles west of Nauvoo. However, things started looking up; that following January, Gudmund Haugaas, himself a Norwegian and a recent Mormon convert in LaSalle County, traveled to visit other Norwegians in Lee County. There he visited the Hogan family and succeeded in baptizing Goudy and his parents.

Now fourteen, Goudy would sometimes row across the Mississippi River to Nauvoo to hear the Prophet Joseph Smith speak. One such occasion was the spring conference of April 6, 1844. Goudy and his father joined a large congregation, and Goudy climbed atop some boards behind the stand to hear better. He was sitting so close to Joseph that he nearly touched his clothes, and it was while there that he noticed a small hole in each of the elbows of the Prophet's linen coat. Goudy remembered thinking that Joseph "was not a proud man and that [this] experience inspired [him] with great confidence and faith that [Joseph] was a great prophet of the Lord."

At one point during the conference, Joseph stopped the elder who was speaking. He rose from his seat and admonished the young men who were flirting loudly in the rear with the young women to not do so. To enforce the directive, he moved through the throng to speak directly to these young men, and the dense crowd parted for him as he passed, "where it would seem impossible for any other man to do so."

Two months later, on June 27, while picking wild strawberries, Goudy heard that Joseph Smith had been martyred. At this news he wept miserably.

Goudy felt the loss of the Prophet for the rest of his days but would always remember his brush with Joseph Smith. He was a lucky boy indeed.

It was Edward Stevenson who said of the Prophet Joseph and his teaching,

> We very often went to Nauvoo to meetings. I have never heard or seen a man so filled with inspiration as the Prophet. He was full of light. I began to believe that he possessed an infinity of knowledge. I looked upon him as upon no other man. I have often heard him speak under divine influence, and I have felt as though I have been lifted in spirit beyond mortality, and that I was looking upon a simile of God, and at times I found myself in tears of joy. Others have I seen in the same condition, and at times even those not members of our church.

Sources

Goudy Hogan, "History of Gaudy Hogan," undated typescript, 2, in the possession of the author.

Goudy Hogan, "Autobiography," undated typescript, ms. 7445, Church History Library, The Church of Jesus Christ of Latter-day Saints, Salt Lake City, Utah, 2.

Hyrum L. Andrus and Helen Mae Andrus, comp., *They Knew the Prophet* (Salt Lake City, Utah: Bookcraft, 1974), 87.

Lydia Goldthwaite Bailey

By William G. Hartley
Retired professor of history, Brigham Young University

In October 1833, Joseph Smith, Sidney Rigdon, and Father Freeman Nickerson traveled to Mount Pleasant, Upper Canada (Ontario), on a missionary journey to preach the gospel to Freeman's two adult sons. The missionary party reached Eleazer Freeman Nickerson's home on October 18, a Friday. The next evening, the host asked Joseph Smith and Sidney Rigdon to explain their religion.

"The Prophet commenced by relating the scenes of his early life. He told how the angel visited him, of his finding the plates, the translation of them, and gave a short account of the matter contained in the Book of Mormon."

Sitting in that audience was a young woman named Lydia Goldthwaite Bailey. She had come to Canada as a guest of the Nickersons. By the tender age of nineteen, she had been married to an abusive, alcoholic husband who had subsequently abandoned her; during their marriage she had given birth to two children, both of whom had died. Lydia had become inconsolable. The Nickersons had invited her to Canada in hopes that a change of scenery would bring back a zest for life. Lydia's biography continues, "As the speaker continued his wonderful narrative, Lydia, who was listening and watching him intently, saw his face become white and a shining glow seemed to beam from every feature."

This witness of the Spirit converted Lydia to Mormonism. Subsequently, on October 27, "twelve came forward and was baptized," including Eleazer Freeman Nickerson, his household, and "Lidia Baeley"—as Joseph Smith spelled her name in his diary. Lydia's biography says she was so thrilled when baptized that she cried out while standing in the cold water, "Glory to God in the highest. Thanks be to His holy name that I have lived to see this day."

The next day at candlelight the believers met, "broke bread," and the missionaries confirmed those who had been baptized. "The spirit was given in great power to some and the rest had great peace," Joseph Smith's journal records. "Had a good meeting. One of the sisters got the gift of tongues, which made the saints rejoice. May God increase the gifts among them for his Son's sake."

That sister was Lydia. In her own account of that meeting, she said that members of the Nickerson family were seated around "the wide, old-fashioned fire-place in the parlor" listening to Joseph Smith teach. Moses Nickerson said he would feel glad if someone who had been baptized "could receive the gift of tongues as the ancient Saints did and speak to us."

Joseph responded that "if one of you will rise up and open your mouth it shall be filled, and you shall speak in tongues." Lydia said that everyone turned to her and urged her to be the one. Then, according to her history,

> she was enveloped as with a flame, and, unable longer to retain her seat, she arose and her mouth was filled with the praises of God and His glory. The spirit of tongues was upon her,

> and she was clothed in shining light, so bright that all present saw it with great distinctness above the light of the fire and the candles.

A revelation earlier had promised Joseph Smith and Sidney Rigdon that the Holy Ghost would be "shed forth" when they taught; Lydia's statement is a testament that the promise was fulfilled.

As Joseph and his party were preparing to return to Kirtland, Joseph Smith paced back and forth in the sitting room, deep in thought. Then, according to Lydia, he said to her and others present:

> I have been pondering on Sister Lydia's lonely condition, and wondering why it is that she has passed through so much sorrow and affliction and is thus separated from all her relatives. I now understand it. The Lord has suffered it even as he allowed Joseph of old to be afflicted, who was sold by his brethren as a slave into a far country, and through that became a savior to his father's house and country. Even so shall it be with her, the hand of the Lord will overrule it for good to her and her father's family.

He then spoke directly to Lydia and pronounced a blessing for her that sounds very much like a patriarchal blessing:

> Sister Lydia, great are your blessings. The Lord, your Savior, loves you and will overrule all your past sorrows and afflictions for good for you. Let your heart be comforted. You are of the blood of Israel descended through the loins of Ephraim. You shall yet be a savior to your father's house.

> Therefore be comforted, and let your heart rejoice, for the Lord has a great work for you to do. Be faithful and endure unto the end and all will be well.

Lydia thereafter gathered to Kirtland, where she met and married Newel Knight. She would remain true and faithful to the end. In 1877, with the opening of the St. George temple, ordinance work for the dead began in earnest in this dispensation. Among those devoted to that work was Lydia Goldthwaite Bailey Knight. Before her death in 1884, she would see to the ordinance work for more than seven hundred of her ancestors and friends—thus fulfilling the Prophet's promise.

Sources

Lydia Knight's History, 18–22.

https://archive.org/stream/lydiaknightshist00gate#page/18/mode/2up/search/joseph+smith.

The Papers of Joseph Smith, 2:10–14.

"Mary Elizabeth, Your Church is Wrong!"

By Mary Jane Woodger
Professor of Church history and doctrine,
Brigham Young University

Mary Elizabeth and Caroline Rollins were the daughters of John D. and Keturah Van Benthuysen Rollins. In 1829, the Rollins family moved to Kirtland, Ohio, where they heard of the Book of Mormon and Joseph Smith and were converted to the gospel. The family then emigrated to Independence, Missouri, in 1831.

Here, Mary Elizabeth worked as a seamstress for Mrs. Lilburn Boggs. One day Mrs. Boggs made her an interesting offer:

> Mary Elizabeth, your Church is wrong. . . . Being a Mormon will only bring you pain and disappointment. . . . My husband has power and money, more than your people do. We want to take you in as one of our own. We will provide for you and educate you. You will be one of us.

Mary Elizabeth refused to "abandon her faith or her people." A few months later, she would witness a mob aroused to rage by her former employer, Lilburn Boggs—who, as the governor of the state of Missouri in 1838, would issue the Mormon extermination order.

This is the kind of courage that the Savior spoke of when He said, "But whosoever shall deny me before men, him will I also deny before my Father which is in heaven" (Matthew 10:32–33).

Sources

Mary E. Lightner, "Mary Elizabeth Rollins Lightner," *The Utah Genealogical and Historical Magazine* 17 (July 1926), 193.

Hillary Watkins Lemon, "A Girl of Great Faith, Part 2: Courage in Independence," *The Friend*, July 2013.

Mary Fielding Smith

By Susan Easton Black
EMERITUS PROFESSOR OF CHURCH HISTORY AND DOCTRINE,
BRIGHAM YOUNG UNIVERSITY

THERE IS GREAT POWER IN prayer, as demonstrated by the story of Mary Fielding Smith.

"When we started out from the Missouri River," Joseph F. Smith recalled, "we had only about one-half enough teams to haul our wagons." Captain Cornelius P. Lott questioned Mary Fielding Smith's preparation to take her family to the Rocky Mountains and suggested that she and her family wait another season before crossing the plains.

According to Joseph F., his mother said to Captain Lott, "I will beat you to the valley and will ask no help from you either." She arrived in the Valley before Captain Lott, but not without difficulty.

While camped near the Missouri River bottoms, Mary's best yoke of oxen wandered off in the night. The next morning, young Joseph F. and his uncle Joseph Fielding searched for the oxen in the tall grass and nearby woods. After several hours of searching, the uncle returned to the encampment "fatigued, disheartened, and almost exhausted."

As young Joseph approached camp, he recalled, "I saw my mother kneeling down to pray. I halted for a moment and then drew gently near enough to hear her pleading with the Lord not to suffer us to be left in this helpless condition, but to lead us to recover our lost team, that we might continue our travels in safety. When she arose from her knees I was standing nearby. The first expression I caught upon her precious face was a lovely smile, which discouraged as I was, gave me renewed hope and an assurance I had not felt before."

"I will just take a walk out and see if I can find the cattle," Mary said to her son.

Joseph watched as she walked toward the riverbank. Before long, she had found the cattle and was calling to him to come and see. Joseph and his uncle started to run. Joseph F. said, "Like John who outran the other disciple to the sepulcher, I outran my uncle and came first to the spot where my mother stood. There I saw our oxen fastened to a clump of willows growing in the bottom of a deep gulch . . . perfectly concealed from view. And we were soon on our way home rejoicing."

Mary's example of humble prayer led Joseph F. to say, "It was one of the first practical and positive demonstrations of the efficacy of prayer I had ever witnessed. It made an indelible impression upon my mind, and has been a source of comfort, assurance and guidance to me throughout all of my life."

Sources

"Cornelius P. Lott," in Leonard J. Arrington and Davis Bitton, *Saints without Halos: The Human Side of Mormon History* (Salt Lake City, Utah: Signature Books, 1982).

Joseph F. Smith, "A Plucky Pioneer Mother," *Improvement Era*, June 1918, 756.

Joseph F. Smith, "How One Widow Crossed the Plains," *Young Woman's Journal*, Feb. 1919, 165.

Joseph Fielding Smith, *Life of Joseph F. Smith: Sixth President of the Church of Jesus Christ of Latter-day Saints* (Salt Lake City, Utah: Deseret News Press, 1938), 131–134.

Andrew Jenson, *Latter-day Saint Biographical Encyclopedia: Compilation of Biographical Sketches of Prominent Men and Women in the Church of Jesus Christ of Latter-day Saints*, 4 vols. (Salt Lake City, Utah: Andrew Jenson History Co., 1901), 1:68.

Messengers of Hope:
Joseph A. Young and Abel Garr

By Andrew Olsen

AUTHOR OF *THE PRICE WE PAID: THE EXTRAORDINARY STORY OF THE WILLIE AND MARTIN HANDCART PIONEERS*

IN THE FALL OF 1856, two handcart companies and two wagon companies—about 1,400 people—were in dire circumstances while still hundreds of miles from Salt Lake City. When President Brigham Young learned that these Saints were late on the trail, he issued an urgent call to rescue them. Two days later, about fifty men with twenty to twenty-five wagons left the city comprising the first rescue team, led by George D. Grant.

Two of these men, Joseph A. Young and Abel Garr, would have a unique role in the rescue. They would be part of every "express" that George Grant sent ahead to find the companies and carry communications. Although Joseph and Abel would bring little food to the famished people, they would bring something just as important, just as real. They would be messengers of hope.

The first rescue team thought they might reach the Willie handcart company within a week. After eight days on the trail, however, they hadn't found them or learned anything about where they might be. "Our hearts began to ache when we reached Green River and yet no word of them," said Daniel W. Jones.

Little did they know that the Willie Saints were still more than 160 miles away, that they had been toiling on reduced rations for more than two weeks, and that they were nearly out of food. The other three companies were yet another 100 miles back on the trail—farther than anyone expected.

With concern escalating, George Grant decided to send express riders to find the people and tell them that help was coming. He selected Joseph Young, Abel Garr, Cyrus Wheelock, and Stephen Taylor for this assignment.

Taking one light wagon, these men raced ahead and finally found the Willie company five days later in a destitute condition. Many were at the point of collapse, but they rallied to greet the men with shouts of joy. The timing of this arrival was providential, coming on the very day the Willie Saints had eaten the last of their flour rations and had been blasted by the first winter storm.

As the people gathered, Joseph Young implored, "Cheer up! Help is coming!" But as he looked into their gaunt, frozen faces, Joseph couldn't hold back his own tears. "Why do you cry, Brother Young?" asked Emily Hill, whom Joseph had known during his mission to England. "Because you look so starved, and the provision wagons are [miles] away," he answered. Joseph then pulled a small onion from his pocket for Emily to eat. The onion was the equivalent of a feast, but instead of eating it, Emily saved it and gave it to a man who appeared to be dying. The man later said that her act of kindness had saved his life.

The express riders had little food to give the four hundred members of the Willie company. Nevertheless, Joseph Elder described the men as "saviors coming to [our] relief," as they revived the people's hopes with the message that wagons loaded with food and clothing were only a day or two away. After staying briefly and giving encouragement, they continued east to search for the last three companies. The Willie Saints shouted cheers of gratitude as the men rode away.

During the next few days, the express traveled to Devil's Gate, 327 miles from Salt Lake City, and still hadn't found the

Martin, Hodgetts, and Hunt companies. George Grant had instructed the men to stop at Devil's Gate, so they waited until the rest of the rescue team arrived. The following day, Grant sent another express to search for the last companies. Again he entrusted Joseph Young and Abel Garr with this assignment, along with Daniel W. Jones.

The three men rode hard and finally found these Saints the next day—some one thousand camped along the Platte River. As the express riders entered the Martin and Hodgetts camp, the frozen, emaciated people came alive to cheer and cry with joy. Sixteen-year-old Albert Jones recalled the scene in vivid detail:

> Joseph A. Young . . . with his big blue soldiers' overcoat, its large cape . . . rising and falling with the motion of the mule, gave the appearance of a big blue-winged angel flying to our rescue. . . . Women and men surrounded him, weeping, and crying aloud; on their knees, holding to the skirts of his coat, as though afraid he would escape from their grasp and fly away. Joseph stood in their midst drawn up to his full height and gazed upon their upturned faces, his eyes full of tears. I, boy as I was, prayed "God bless him."

Members of the Martin handcart company were in even worse condition than the Willie company had been. After the first storm nine days earlier, they had soon become too weak to travel, and for the previous six days they had been mired in the snow at Red Buttes. Fifty-six had died since the first storm. Many more were near death, barely subsisting on a handful of flour a day.

Again the express had little food to give, but their news that provision wagons were only about fifty miles away gave the people hope. Joseph Young said they must "gather up and move on," impossible as that seemed, "as the only salvation was to travel a little every day." The three men then left to find the Hunt company, which was camped about ten miles downriver.

The next day the express riders helped the companies get started, and the day after that they hurried back to Devil's Gate, arriving after dark to report on the desperate plight of the people. "All were rejoiced to get the news that we had found the emigrants," Daniel Jones said. Early the next morning, most of George Grant's team started east, and that evening they met the Martin company and distributed life-saving food and clothing. Abel Garr and a few others helped pull some of the handcarts the last couple of miles to where the rescuers had built big fires. "We were very thankful," said Louisa Mellor. "The overwhelming feeling we had cannot be described."

The five hundred members of the Martin company needed two more grueling days to reach Devil's Gate. The rescuers assisted all they could, but George Grant said his small team "was only a drop to a bucket . . . in comparison to what is needed." In a letter to Brigham Young, he wrote that the handcart Saints were "fainting by the wayside; falling, chilled by the cold; children crying, their limbs stiffened by cold, their feet bleeding and some of them bare to snow and frost. The sight is almost too much for the stoutest of us." Daniel Jones noted another problem: "The provisions we had brought from Salt Lake City . . . amounted to almost nothing distributed among so many people."

George Grant needed to send his letter to Brigham Young as quickly as possible to inform him of the crisis and to seek help. Once again he chose Joseph Young and Abel Garr for a risky, crucial express mission. These men had been traveling express nearly nonstop for more than three weeks. As they prepared to leave, Joseph put on a few pairs of wool socks, along with some buffalo-hide overshoes, and said, "If my feet freeze with those on, they must stay frozen till I get to Salt Lake."

Riding through storm after storm, Joseph and Abel traveled the 327 miles to Salt Lake City in ten days, arriving at 4 a.m. on November 13. Along the way, they turned around many rescuers who had given up the search and were on their way home. After delivering George Grant's letter and reporting on the last companies, they went back to the mountains to break the trail through waist-deep snow.

* * * *

Although Joseph Young and Abel Garr brought little physical assistance to the pioneers they found freezing and starving on the plains, they were messengers of hope. That hope had a sustaining power beyond any reasonable expectation—and was essential in helping more than 1,100 members of these late companies survive their ordeal.

Abel Garr was not a member of the Church at the time of the rescue. He was baptized and confirmed the next year by members of the rescue team.

Fifty-one years after the rescue, Robert T. Burton, who had been an assistant to George Grant, wrote a letter to the Handcart Veterans' Association in which he highlighted the service of Joseph Young, Abel Garr, and the other express riders:

> I cannot leave this subject without expressing thanks to those brave men who were constant day and night in their efforts to save the people, and more especially do I wish to remember those who endangered their lives to carry expresses, east and west, under the most difficult circumstances. Notable among these were: Joseph A. Young, Steven Taylor, C. H. Wheelock, Abel Garr and Dan Jones, most of whom have passed away. Of

> course, too much credit cannot be given to the entire [rescue] company for their indefatigable labors night and day.

Sources

1. Daniel W. Jones, *Forty Years among the Indians* (1960), 62.
2. Betsey Smith Goodwin, "The Tired Mother: Pioneer Recollections," *Improvement Era*, July 1919, 779.
3. Mary F. Kelly, "Emily Hill Woodmansee, Poetess," *Young Woman's Journal*, Feb. 1907, 52.
4. Joseph Elder journal, 21, Church History Library; see also William Woodward, in Willie company journal appendix, 53, Church History Library. The rescue wagons arrived to assist the Willie company three days after the express arrived—and after a heroic effort by James Willie and Joseph Elder to find them.
5. Albert Jones, "Utah Heroes Who Pulled Their All across the Plains," *Deseret Evening News*, Sept. 1, 1906, 20.
6. See James G. Bleak journal, Oct. 28, 1856, Church History Library;
7. Jones, 65.
8. Jones, 67.
9. Louisa Mellor Clark, "History of Louisa Mellor Clark," given at Spring Lake, Utah, Mar. 26, 1881, 4, Daughters of Utah Pioneers History Department.
10. George D. Grant, "The Companies Yet on the Plains," *Deseret News*, Nov. 19, 1856, 293.
11. Jones, 68.
12. In John Jaques, *Salt Lake Daily Herald*, Dec. 15, 1878, 1.
13. Robert T. Burton letter, Oct. 1, 1907, in Handcart Veterans' Association Scrapbook, folder 4, Church History Library.

Mighty Prayer

By Glenn Rawson

STORYTELLER ON THE *SOUNDS OF SUNDAY* RADIO PROGRAM

THERE IS PRAYER, AND THEN there is what the Lord calls "mighty prayer" (D&C 29:2). What follows could not be more of an example of that kind of prayer.

It was called the exodus of Kirtland—in early 1838, the enemies of the Church finally became so violent and threatening that many of the Saints were forced to flee. It was January 12 when Joseph Smith was warned of the Lord and left Kirtland in the middle of the night. Others followed as they could and made their way toward Missouri.

One family had a particularly difficult time. The patriarch of the family, an old man of sixty-six, was harassed by bogus lawsuits and forced to hide. In fear for his life, he ran from town to town and house to house for months to avoid his enemies. Finally all was in readiness, and he reunited with his family as they fled west to join the Saints in Far West, Missouri.

The company with which they united was a large company, and the going was particularly slow, made worse by the weather. The mother spoke of a time when they lay all night exposed to the rain until they were soaked through. The next day it was fruitless to change into dry clothes, for the rain continued to fall. For three days they trudged on, cold, soaked, and weary, until the mother was taken with a severe cold and a violent cough. By the time they reached the Mississippi River, she was so ill she unable to walk or sit up.

To compound the already difficult circumstances, one married daughter, Catherine, went into labor; she delivered a baby boy in a squalid hut near the river. All of this combined to render the family unable to travel.

A couple of days later, while the family was away, the aging mother set her mind that she needed to pray somewhere where she would not be interrupted. Some distance from the house was a dense thicket that would afford the privacy she sought. Accordingly, she took a staff in each hand and by that assistance was enabled to reach the thicket. As soon as she had caught her breath so as to speak with ease, she commenced praying for her health and that of her daughter. She called upon every promise of scripture that she could think of and continued praying faithfully for three hours. The Lord heard her. The wracking cough left her, and she was made well.

She made her way back to her family and learned that her daughter was similarly ready to travel.

The family of Joseph Smith Sr. soon went on their way and arrived safely in Far West. That mother determined to pray was Lucy Mack Smith.

It was Amulek who declared, "Thou art merciful unto thy children when they cry unto thee to be heard of thee and not of men, and thou wilt hear them" (Alma 33:8). And indeed He will!

Source

Lucy Mack Smith, *History of Joseph by His Mother* (Salt Lake City, Utah: Deseret Book, 2009), 251–253.

Miracle at the Missouri River: Coins in a Fish

By Alexander L. Baugh

Professor of Church history and doctrine,
Brigham Young University

In the New Testament, Matthew recorded a most unusual miracle performed by Jesus. On one occasion, Peter was asked by the religious leaders if Jesus complied with the law of Moses, which stipulated that all males over the age of twenty pay an annual "tribute," or tax, that was used to maintain the temple in Jerusalem. When Peter asked Jesus about the payment, he told Peter to go fishing and upon catching the first fish, open its mouth and he would find the coin necessary to make the payment (see Matthew 17:24–27). Significantly, a similar incident occurred in early LDS Church history.

In early November 1833, the citizens of Jackson County, Missouri, came out in open opposition against the Mormons and forced them to leave the county. Most of the approximately twelve hundred Latter-day Saints sought refuge in Clay County, situated across the Missouri River directly north of Jackson. However, some families, like that of John and Keturah Rollins, lacked the means to pay the cost of the ferry, leaving them temporarily stranded.

Fifteen year-old Mary Elizabeth Rollins later recalled the miracle that enabled her family and several others to make their way across the river. She wrote: "While we were camped on the banks of the Missouri River waiting to be ferried over, they found there was not money enough to take all over. So, some of the brethren . . . thought they would try and catch some fish, perhaps the ferryman would take them." She continued, "They put out their lines in the evening; it rained all night and most of the next day, when they took in their lines they found two or three small fish, and a catfish that weighed 14 pounds. On opening it, what was their astonishment to find three bright silver half dollars, just the amount needed to pay for taking their team over the river. This was considered a miracle, and caused great rejoicing among us."

Nephi said, "I, Nephi, will show unto you that the tender mercies of the Lord are over all those whom he hath chosen, because of their faith, to make them mighty even unto the power of deliverance" (1 Nephi 1:20). And the Lord is still showing this among the faithful.

Source

Mary Elizabeth Rollins Lightner, "Mary Elizabeth Rollins Lightner," *The Utah Genealogical and Historical Magazine* 17 (July 1926), 197.

Miracle of the Quail

By Glenn Rawson

Writer, producer, and host of the *Joseph Smith Papers* and *History of the Saints* television series

It was October 9, 1846, at Potter's Slough on the Mississippi River's west bank. Thomas Bullock and others of the poorest of the Latter-day Saints were gathering what meager belongings they had and preparing to forever turn their backs on their beloved city of Nauvoo.

They had been driven out of Nauvoo and across the river by angry, hateful mobs. They had been beaten, abused, and threatened. Several were mockingly "baptized" in the river in the name of the murdered Prophet, Joseph Smith. Their city and homes were ransacked and looted by the mob and their sacred temple had been desecrated. Even the angel and ball on its top had been pilfered.

It was growing late in the season. The nights were cold. They had little food, insufficient clothing, and meager shelter. Some were determined to reach the main body of the Saints three hundred miles to the west on the Missouri, and they set out, leaving the poorest of the poor huddled in a filthy swamp. They had seventeen tents and eight wagons with no oxen to pull them. Thomas Bullock was one of these. He was sick with lingering chills and fever and scarcely able to get around, yet he was a faithful record keeper.

Then, from the West, Captain Orville Allen came into camp with several wagons and a mandate to rescue as many of the stranded Saints as possible. He organized them, gathered up what little they had, and instructed them. If they had sufficient means, they would go directly to Winter Quarters, but if not they would stop and work until they did.

On the morning of October 9, 1846, Captain Allen called all the men out who were well at the cock's crow and ordered them to build fires and prepare breakfast. Thomas Bullock arose with a terrible headache, and then it happened—several large flocks of quail flew into the camp, lighting on the wagons, the ground, and even on their breakfast tables. The men and boys ran about and caught them. The quail would lift off, fly around briefly, and once more land in the camp, allowing the suffering exiles to catch them easily. Thomas Bullock recorded, "This morning we had a direct manifestation of the mercy and goodness of God in a miracle being performed in the camp . . ."

He describes the quail alighting and then wrote, "The brethren and sisters praised God and glorified his name, that what was showered down upon the Children of Israel in the wilderness is manifested unto us in our persecution."

That day, every man, woman and child in the camp had plenty to eat. To the astonishment of all, the quail continued to circle the camp throughout the day. At four-thirty that afternoon, Captain Allen gave the order, and Bullock and the others began their journey to a new home somewhere in the West.

As he left this scene of miracles, Bullock wrote, "I left the banks of the Mississippi, my property, Nauvoo, and the mob forever, and started merrily over a level prairie, amid the songs of quails and blackbirds, the Sun shining smilingly upon us. . . . The scene was delightful. . . . All things conspired for us to praise the Lord."

Sources

Orville M. Allen Journal, Oct. 9, 1846.
Thomas Bullock Journal, Oct. 9, 1846.

Mother Whitmer and the Angel

By Glenn Rawson

STORYTELLER ON THE *SOUNDS OF SUNDAY* RADIO PROGRAM

IT IS A TRUE PRINCIPLE that the Lord will try the faith of his people in order that they might prove their faithfulness. Such a thing took place in one of the most sacred sites of Mormonism—the Peter Whitmer Cabin in Fayette, New York. It was there that the Book of Mormon translation was completed. It was there that three men were chosen as special witnesses and granted the opportunity to converse with an angel, view the plates, and hear the witness of God in regard to the Book of Mormon. It was also there that The Church of Jesus Christ of Latter-day Saints was organized on April 6, 1830, and many other great revelations were received. Considering the incalculable souls eternally blessed by what happened there, truly this is a holy place where the mercy of God was abundant.

But there was a day when this glorious future almost didn't happen. Joseph Smith came to Fayette in June 1829 at the encouragement of Peter and Mary Whitmer. It was their generosity that opened up an upper room in which to translate. It was the food at their table and a place to sleep that sustained life while the work progressed.

With Joseph came Emma and Oliver Cowdery, as well as an innumerable train of visitors and the curious. All of it increased the burden on Mother Whitmer, who felt the responsibility to care for all of them.

One day Mother Whitmer was particularly tired. She went outside to attend the evening chores and milk the cow. She saw Joseph and Oliver nearby skating rocks across the pond—an activity they often did to relax and relieve the tedium of translation. The sight annoyed her, and she thought to herself that they might just as well chop some wood or carry a bucket of water as skip rocks. According to her family, she was so annoyed that she was about to order them from the home.

At that point, coming out of the barn and carrying two buckets of milk, she was met by a stranger—a heavyset old man with a knapsack on his back. At first she was frightened, but

> when he spoke to her in a kind, friendly tone and began to explain to her the nature of the work which was going on in her house, she was filled with inexpressible joy and satisfaction. He then untied his knapsack and showed her a bundle of plates, which in size and appearance corresponded with the description subsequently given by the witnesses to the Book of Mormon. This strange person turned the leaves of the book of plates over, leaf after leaf, and also showed her the engravings upon them; after which he told her to be patient and faithful in bearing her burden a little longer, promising that if she would do so, she should be blessed; and her reward would be sure, if she proved faithful to the end. The personage then suddenly vanished with the plates, and where he

> went, she could not tell. From that moment [Mother Whitmer] was enabled to perform her household duties with comparative ease, and she felt no more inclination to murmur because her lot was hard.

Sources

Royal Skousen, "Another Account of Mary Whitmer's Viewing of the Golden Plates," *Interpreter: A Journal of Mormon Scripture* 10 (2014), 35–44.

http://www.deseretnews.com/article/865583267/Mary-Whitmer-12th-witness-to-the-Book-of-Mormon.html?pg=all

Ole and Marn

By Glenn Rawson

Writer, producer, and host of the *Joseph Smith Papers* and *History of the Saints* television series

How does the Lord most often speak to his people? By the still, small voice of the Spirit—by thoughts, feelings, and impressions—as illustrated in the experience of the Petersons.

Ole and Marn Peterson had left Denmark in April 1857, bound for Utah. Once in America they had been assigned to the Park handcart company. However, at the Missouri River, Marn was told she would never make it because of an infection in her leg. The couple stayed near Council Bluffs and farmed, preparing for that day when they could continue on to Zion. Then, in the spring of 1861, a large wagon train was organized; Ole and Marn and their four children—Peder, age fourteen; Annie, age six; and the babies, Mary and Joseph—joined with them.

Somewhere along the trail, sickness spread through the camp, and Annie became ill. Despite the fact that she was administered to and fervent prayers were offered on her behalf, Annie grew weaker until at last she was declared dead. Because of danger on the trail from Indians, it was decreed that the company had to move on and there was not time to dig a proper grave. According to family records, the child was wrapped in a blanket and covered in heavy brush.

Death was no stranger to Ole and Marn; they had already buried three children in their native Denmark. Nevertheless, it was hard to leave Annie behind. Obediently they went on. They had not gone far when it was deemed expedient to make camp, as Indians threatened.

That night around the fire, as was customary, the company sang, "Come, Come Ye Saints," the anthem of the trail. As they raised their voices to sing "All is well, all is well!" the feeling gnawed at Marn that all was not well. It was like the Spirit was trying to tell her something.

"Ole," she said, "I can't feel our baby was dead."

"I know, dear," Ole gently replied. "We had so many plans, but she was, and there is nothing we can do now but pray that we will be able to raise the family we have, and more when we settle in Zion. Come to the wagon so you will be refreshed for tomorrow's travel."

Weary, Marn started for the wagon.

"Ole, listen to the wolves, and our baby is lying back there alone, not even protected by a grave. How can we stand to go on?"

"We must make up our minds to go on and trust in the Lord for the rest," he replied.

"I can't, Ole! I just can't!" Marn cried.

Gently but firmly, Ole took her by the arm and led her back to their wagon.

The next morning at dawn, Ole discovered that Marn was not in her bed and nowhere to be found in the camp. A search was mounted until suddenly someone spotted her in the distance coming toward camp from the east. She was carrying a burden and stumbling with weariness.

Ole ran to his wife and lifted the burden from her arms. As he spoke to Marn, it struck him that the burden was Annie—

and she was alive. Annie Christina Peterson would recover and live to marry Samuel Wilcox, bear nine children, and as a midwife bring many children safely into mortality.

The Lord promised Oliver and all of us, "Behold, I will tell you in your mind and in your heart by the Holy Ghost which shall come upon you and which shall dwell in your heart" (D&C 8:2).

Source

Donald Long History at https://familysearch.org/photos/stories/ 2875272.

Oliver's Return

By Glenn Rawson

STORYTELLER ON THE *SOUNDS OF SUNDAY* RADIO PROGRAM

OLIVER COWDERY WAS A MAN highly favored of the Lord. He was granted a vision to know that the Book of Mormon was true even before he met Joseph Smith. He wrote the translation of nearly the entire Book of Mormon as it fell from the lips of the Prophet. He received the Aaronic Priesthood under the hand of John the Baptist and the Melchizedek Priesthood from Peter, James and John. He saw in vision the glories these two priesthoods would work down through time.

He was the first man baptized for the remission of sins in this dispensation and was the Second Elder in the Church. He stood in the presence of the Lord Jesus Christ in the Kirtland Temple and, with Joseph, received the keys of the kingdom from Moses, Elias, and Elijah.

But then in 1838, Oliver became angry with the government of the Church and what he considered the unjust behavior of certain officers. He was called before the high council to answer a number of charges against him. On the basis of principle and pride, Oliver refused to appear and was excommunicated. At this critical moment other men, angry with the Church, approached Oliver and asked him candidly if he really had seen the plates and the angel. To their surprise, he affirmed that the testimony written in the Book of Mormon was true. Oliver may have been angry, but he was not an apostate.

For ten and a half years, Oliver was outside the Church. He practiced law in Ohio as the Church moved on. He maintained favorable relations with friends in the Church and strived diligently to maintain a reputation worthy of what he had witnessed.

As time passed, Oliver's heart softened. He spoke in his correspondence of being the oldest member of the Church and of returning to the Church and going west. Finally, on October 27, 1848, Oliver rode into a clearing near Kanesville, Iowa, in the middle of a Church conference. He was brought to the stand and invited to speak. With great emotion he took the pulpit and spoke to the largest audience he had ever addressed. He bore a powerful and compelling witness of what he knew of a certainty:

> Friends and Brethren, my name is Cowdery—Oliver Cowdery. In the early history of this Church I stood identified with her, and one in her councils. . . . I wrote, with my own pen, the entire Book of Mormon (save a few pages), as it fell from the lips of the Prophet Joseph Smith, as he translated it by the gift and power of God, by the means of the Urim and Thummim, or, as it is called by that book, "holy interpreters." I beheld with my eyes and handled with my hands the gold plates from which it was translated. I also saw with my eyes and handled with my hands the "holy interpreters." That book is true. Sidney Rigdon did not write it. Mr. Spaulding did not write it. I wrote it myself as it fell from the lips of the Prophet.

On November 12, 1848, Oliver was rebaptized, but before he could go west he was taken sick. As he died, Oliver said, "Now I lay me down for the last time. I am going to my Savior." It was said that he died the happiest of men.

Thank God for the unspeakable gift of repentance. "I, the Lord, forgive sins, and am merciful unto those who confess their sins with humble hearts" (D&C 61:2).

Sources

Richard Lloyd Anderson, *Investigating the Book of Mormon Witnesses* (Salt Lake City, Utah: Shadow Mountain, 2000), 36–65.

The Contributor, vol. 5, no. 11, Aug. 1884.

Patty Bartlett Sessions

By Susan Easton Black
EMERITUS PROFESSOR OF CHURCH HISTORY AND DOCTRINE,
BRIGHAM YOUNG UNIVERSITY

BY THE JOURNAL WE KEEP so will history remember us and our times—something that is clearly demonstrated in the story of Patty Bartlett Sessions.

The rich life of Patty Sessions might have been lost to future generations, never to become a tale of embellished folklore, had she not accepted a simple gift—a small notebook. The inscription on the notebook reads, "A Day Book, given to me, Patty Sessions, by Sylvia . . . this 10th day of February, 1846. Patty Sessions, her book. I am now fifty-one years, six days old. February 10, 1846, City of Joseph, Hancock County, Illinois."

In her daybook, Patty recorded her inner thoughts, never realizing that her words would one day be an inspiration to future generations. Although her literary talents pale in comparison to those of friend and poetess Eliza R. Snow, Patty's day-to-day notations on the westward Mormon trek tell of a woman who had faith in Jesus Christ and enjoyed the mercies of God in the face of difficult, even insurmountable, challenges.

Of her willingness to be a follower of Christ, Patty penned, "I desire to do right and live my religion that I may enjoy the light to see as I am seen and know as I am known. O my Father, help me to live my religion, this is my greatest desire." By centering her life on Jesus Christ, Patty found abiding happiness. "I am happy all the time," she penned. Even when her happiness was tested as she traversed the loamy hills of Iowa, she wrote, "I have been in the cold and in the mud. There is no food for our teams. I never have felt so bad as now, but I am not discouraged yet . . . although alone by myself I am happy."

Patty noted that her happiness increased as she gave of herself to heal the sick on the Mormon trek. On March 6, 1846, she penned, "I go back ten miles this morning to see Sarah Ann. She was sick. Sent for me. I rode horseback." She later recorded, "Was sent for to go back two miles to a sick woman, Sister Stewart. I asked her [for] no pay." There is no hint of self-pity or resentment in her diary entries for the time or sacrifice she spent in the service of others.

By her daily entries, Patty revealed that seemingly insignificant notations about a life of faith and service can change an ordinary, too easily forgotten life into a saga of grand proportions. By recording the ordinary, Patty showed that her journey to find happiness and receive the mercies of God was to live a Christ-centered life. Through simple notations, she taught that the campfire hymn "Come, Come, Ye Saints" was not merely a pleasing refrain but was her way of life. She concluded, "I feel to thank the Lord that I have passed through what I have. I have gained an experience I could not have gained no other way."

In December 1980, President Spencer W. Kimball said, "I promise you that if you will keep your journals and records, they will indeed be a source of great inspiration to your families, to your children, your grandchildren, and others, on through the generations."

Sources

Patty Bartlett Sessions, daybook, in Claire Augusta Wilcox Noall, *Guardians of the Hearth: Utah's Pioneer Midwives and Women Doctors* (Bountiful, Utah: Horizon Publishers, 1974), 22.

Elizabeth Willis, "Voice in the Wilderness: The Diaries of Patty Sessions," *Journal of American Folklore* (Boston: Houghton Mifflin, 1988), 45.

https://www.lds.org/new-era/1980/12/president-kimball-speaks-out-on-personal-journals?lang=eng.

Promise to Charles Henry

By Glenn Rawson

Storyteller on the *Sounds of Sunday* radio programs

Ann had already lost several of her children to death, so when little Charles Henry became ill she worried for him. Many families in the area had lost children to some mysterious cause. Would Charles be next? In time, Charles slipped into a coma. Ann called for the doctor, but he told her that nothing could be done for the boy. He had only a few hours left to live. Before the physician left, he completed a death certificate for Charles and signed it so he wouldn't have to come back later. He showed Ann where to fill in the hour of death and instructed her to have it registered later.

But Ann could not give up so easily. With faith and prayers she clung to the child. As she prayed, the elders came to the door. She welcomed them with open arms and asked them to administer to her son. They laid their hands on his head and promised in the name of the Lord that he would be healed. Then they continued—they promised that in due time he would go to Zion, and that in a coming day he would be called as a missionary and sent back to his native Wales. The blessing closed and the elders departed.

Shortly after, Charles Henry suddenly awakened, sat up, and asked for something to eat.

Ann kept all these things in her heart and told no one. In time, true to the promise, the family immigrated to America and took up residence in Vernal, Utah. Then, in the spring of 1897, an unexpected letter came for Charles Henry. It was from Salt Lake City, the office of President Wilford Woodruff. It was a call to serve as a missionary in Europe. The call did not specify where he would serve, nor did his local stake and ward authorities know anything of the call. They hadn't recommended him, but the call had come anyway.

Ann then told Charles of that day so many years before when she had held his death certificate and heard the promises of God pronounced upon his head. "You will go," she said. "This blessing shall be fulfilled. The Lord will prepare the way. He never makes a promise without keeping it."

On October 25, 1897, Charles Henry Davies, along with a large group of missionaries, arrived in Liverpool, England. Shortly after, they stood before Elder Rulon S. Wells. Each was asked where he would like to serve, and each voiced his preference and was assigned. Charles remained silent. Finally Elder Wells turned to Charles—the last one—and told him that he seemed to be something of a lost sheep. Then Elder Wells closed his eyes, and after a moment opened them and said, "The only place I see for you is to the Welsh conference."

The next morning, Charles, the boy given up for dead so many years earlier, left for his native Wales. He would live until 1954, and the promises stood fulfilled.

Source

Hemsley Family History.

"Put Me Down For $2.50"

By Steven M. Parkin
Civil Engineer

The faith of William J. Parkin and his wife, Eliza Foulds, sometimes harmonious and sometimes awry, strengthened the other when one was weak. These two immigrants, who both arrived in Utah from England in 1863 and married a year later, often exercised faith at divergent seasons. Faith lifted one when faith in the other was low.

Though very poor, they acquired a piece of land in South Bountiful, Utah, to work on a share system. In England, William had been a coal miner and knew little about farming, which skill he slowly acquired by experience.

Meanwhile, at the Church conference in Salt Lake City the spring after he was married, William heard President Brigham Young ask for a cash collection to help the immigrant poor come to Zion.

At a meeting the following Sunday, Bishop John Stoker of Bountiful began to take pledges for the campaign. Unsure as to how he would raise the money, William Parkin was the first to stand and volunteer. "Bishop, you may put me down for $2.50."

When William arrived home, his wife met him at the gate, having already heard from neighbors of the foolish pledge. The day before the money was due, William, still penniless, saw near the chicken coop a narrow path leading into a thicket. Following it, he found a large nest of eggs. Gathering his treasure, he returned to the house to meet Eliza, who showed him an unusually large chunk of butter she had churned that morning.

While they were still reflecting upon their good fortune, an overland traveler on his way to California knocked at the door. Food being scarce in the Territory of Utah at the time, the stranger pleaded that after being turned away so many times, he badly needed butter, eggs, and milk. He said he would pay well for them. William and Eliza accepted the stranger's offer. The traveler paid William with a small coin William had never seen before—a $2.50 gold piece.

Though the gold coin was far too much payment for the butter and eggs, the traveler said the food was worth it to him because he was so short of supplies. The following day, grateful for his own generosity and faithful promptings, William was the first to fulfill his pledge to Bishop Stoker. Eliza "assured him that she would never more reproach him" for doing his duty as a Latter-day Saint.

A few years later, as a potato farmer with a failed crop of only very small potatoes, Brother Parkin was embarrassed to pay tithing with them. He decided he would wait until the following year and pay double when he had a better crop. Eliza did not approve and urged him to swallow his pride and pay ten percent of his present harvest. He refused.

The next year he worked harder with a larger patch of potatoes, hoping to get a good harvest with which to pay tithing for both years. At first, the crop looked promising, but to his disappointment, the harvest was well below average. Eliza said, "Now go and buy three bushels of the best potatoes you can get, and turn them in for tithing, and ask the Lord to forgive you."

Eliza's faith prevailed; she lived until 1889 and never saw another crop failure on their land.

It is well to be reminded what the Lord said, for it is the essence of faith itself: "Trust in the Lord with all thine heart; and lean not unto thine own understanding. In all thy ways acknowledge him, and he shall direct thy paths" (Proverbs 3:5).

Source

George C. Lambert, comp., *Gems of Reminiscence, Seventeenth Book of the Faith-Promoting Series* (Salt Lake City, Utah: Geo. C. Lambert, 1915), 33, 36.

Robert Gardner Jr.

By Steven L. Olsen
Senior curator for historic sites,
The Church of Jesus Christ of Latter-day Saints

One of the most oft-repeated commandments in the beginning of this dispensation was, "Seek to bring forth and establish the cause of Zion" (D&C 11:6). This call from the Lord remains in effect and has taken our people to the very ends of the earth.

One of those was Robert Gardner, a founder of several settlements in Utah's "Dixie." He served the Church as a bishop, stake president, and patriarch and served the city of St. George as mayor. His posterity is numerous, his legacy exemplary. But several circumstances in his life almost prevented this eventual destiny. Rather than stop him, they strengthened him and helped him establish a heritage of faithfulness to the Lord and service to family, community, and Church.

Robert was born in 1819 in Scotland. Twenty-five years later he was baptized a member of The Church of Jesus Christ of Latter-day Saints by his brother William and ordained an elder. That same year he moved with his young family from eastern Canada to the Mormon settlement of Nauvoo, Illinois, a distance of about a thousand miles.

Two years later, Robert and his family immigrated to the Great Basin with one of the first companies of Mormon pioneers and settled in the Mill Creek area of the Great Salt Lake Valley. There Robert established a grist mill and a saw mill.

One winter, Robert climbed the steep, snow-covered mountain above the saw mill to bring felled trees down to the mill, not realizing that other men had preceded him on the same errand. Without warning, a large log came down the saw mill's flume. It struck him in the right leg, removing a large portion of flesh from his calf—clear to the bone. Bleeding profusely and in terrible pain, he crawled to a place where he got the attention of two men who took him to his home. On the way, he found in his boot the severed portion of his leg and wrapped it against the open wound with his handkerchief.

Porter Rockwell brought him some whiskey and molasses to clean the wound and deaden the pain. At Robert's home, Porter thoroughly washed the wound, cauterized the blood vessels with salt, and began to reattach the piece of flesh with silk thread. Soon, however, Porter's "heart failed him." So, according to Robert's journal, those who were assisting with the operation "held me and I sewed it myself." He added, "We made a good job of it."

A year later, Robert was not completely healed but felt well enough to accept a call to serve a Church mission in eastern Canada. Robert and his seventy-five fellow missionaries began walking the entire way, pulling handcarts packed with all their belongings. Near Omaha, Nebraska, they were called home because of the advance of Johnston's Army and the threat of conflict in Utah.

After walking more than a thousand miles back to Salt Lake City, Robert participated in the evacuation south to protect the defenseless Saints from the advancing armies. As trying as this time was for him and his family, Robert felt "thankful to God for his blessing in sparing me on my mission, and blessing my family while I was gone." Of this period, when his three wives and many children lived together, Robert later reflected, "This was the happiest time of my life, for all was peace and good feelings."

During this time of well-being, Robert received word that he had been called by Church President Brigham Young to join the Cotton Mission in southern Utah. He later wrote about his immediate reaction to this unexpected news: "I looked and spat, took off my hat, scratched my head, thought, and said, 'All right.'" He arranged his family and business affairs, and left for Dixie with a portion of his family on November 12, 1861, picking up a missionary companion, William Lang, in Provo.

Traveling south through a difficult winter, the missionaries were often denied food and lodging for their families and livestock. On one occasion, however, a resident asked them who they were and where they were from. After hearing Robert's responses, the man said, "Take all your animals into my stable and feed them all they want. I went to your house [in Mill Creek] one night to inquire my way to my uncles on the Church farm. You told me the way, but said, 'It is too late to go there tonight. Stay here all night and I will show you the way in the morning.' He said, 'You gave me my supper and breakfast and a bed and would not charge me a cent. So you and brother Lang must have all you want, for I have plenty.'"

They continued their journey, soon met up with other missionaries who preceded them, and made their way to Dixie, where they laid the foundations of several settlements and the Church.

Sources

"Robert Gardner, Utah Pioneer, 1847," typescript, Church History Library.

Celestia Snow Gardner, *History of the William Snow and Robert Gardner Families, Pioneers of 1847 and 1850* (Salt Lake City, Utah: Acord Printing Co., 1942).

Robert and Mary Henderson

By Kenneth L. Alford

A THIRD GREAT-GRANDSON

MARY ROSS WAS BORN ON August 17, 1823, near Penston, Scotland. Her husband, Robert Henderson, was born in Penston on March 17, 1825, near the east coast of Scotland. Penston and the surrounding villages were coal mining towns, and Robert made his living working in the mines. To help make ends meet, Mary also occasionally worked in the mines.

Latter-day Saint missionaries visited sometime before April 1849. Mary asked Robert if she could attend a cottage meeting and listen to the missionaries preach. Robert counseled her not to attend. Mary was a devoted wife, but she also deeply wanted to listen to the missionaries. When a friend invited her to attend a cottage meeting, she figured out a way to go but still obey Robert's counsel. She stayed outside (so she did not technically attend the meeting) and listened to the meeting through the keyhole. She later reported that she felt the Spirit of the Lord immediately and was in tears before the completion of the first hymn. She returned to her home that evening desiring to be baptized. Robert consented, and she was baptized on April 1, 1849.

Mary persuaded Robert to investigate her new religion, and he too became converted to the restored gospel of Jesus Christ and was baptized on May 19, 1849. During his confirmation blessing, Robert was promised that he would travel to America with his wife and children to gather with the Saints in Utah. He went home deeply concerned about his confirmation blessing. He said that no one could promise such a thing and expect it to come true. He was a poor miner, and it was all he could to do keep food on the table for his family. He believed that immigrating to America, while a wonderful dream, was absolutely out of the question. He accepted leadership callings and served the Church in the Penston area.

One evening Robert came home and told his wife that there was a lot of illness among the workers in his mine because of bad air. Many of the miners were refusing to work. To remedy the problem, his company had called for bids to dig a new air shaft so the mine could reopen.

Mary insisted that he should submit a bid, which he reluctantly did. Afterward, he became angry and reminded Mary that he had no experience doing that kind of work and did not even have any tools with which to do the job. To his consternation, his bid was selected, and he was now obligated to dig the new shaft.

He had no idea how to begin, but Mary insisted that he must try. So he borrowed a pick and shovel and started digging a hole in the ground over the mine. He continued digging, throwing the dirt back over his head until the hole was a little deeper than he was tall. He was quickly reaching the point where he could no longer throw the dirt out of the hole, yet he still had several hundred feet to dig until he would reach the mine shaft below.

Just as he was reaching the point when he could no longer throw dirt out of the hole, he struck a fault in the earth—a crack that extended from where he was and into the mine shaft below. The fault sent more air into the mine than a regular air shaft could have provided. The mining company was so pleased that they paid Robert the full amount promised in his bid—even though he had worked for just a brief period.

Robert and Mary now had sufficient money to immigrate to the United States. They sailed from Liverpool, England, on May 30, 1863, on the ship Cynosure. After arriving in the United States on July 19, 1863, they made their way to Utah—as Robert had been promised.

"It is my purpose to provide for my saints, for all things are mine" (D&C 104:15). And He continues to provide.

Source

Unpublished family histories of Robert Henderson and Mary Ross Henderson, in the possession of the author.

Sallie Heller Conrad

By Glenn Rawson

STORYTELLER ON THE *SOUNDS OF SUNDAY* RADIO PROGRAM

UNDOUBTEDLY WHEN SALLY TOOK THE job, she hadn't planned on this. She was eighteen years old and hired to help out a busy mother around the house. The home was small, and in addition to the large family already living there, there were also guests living at the house.

Something was going on upstairs. One day Sally noticed a couple of young men coming down from the second story. They looked most unusual. Their faces were "exceedingly white and strange." She asked the family why they looked that way, but no one would tell her. It was like the family was keeping some kind of mysterious secret.

As time passed, it happened again and again. Each time Sally saw them, their faces were that same unearthly white. Finally she went to the lady of the house and announced "that she would not stay with her until she knew the cause of the strange looks of these men."

The lady of that house was Mother Mary Whitmer of Fayette, New York. It was June 1829. Mother Whitmer explained to Sally that those two men—Joseph Smith and Oliver Cowdery—were translating an ancient record written upon gold plates by the gift and power of God, and "that the power of God was so great in the room that they could hardly endure it; at times angels were in the room in their glory, which nearly consumed them."

Mother Whitmer's explanation satisfied the girl and opened the way to Sally embracing the gospel.

Sallie Heller Conrad married in the faith, came west, and died in Provo, Utah, on July 23, 1903. She was ninety-two years old.

Just as the skin of Moses's face shone to the wonder and amazement of Israel (see Exodus 34:35), so it is just as wonderful when the Lord's servants are transfigured in these days.

Source

Mark L. McConkie, *Remembering Joseph: Personal Recollections of Those Who Knew the Prophet Joseph Smith* (Salt Lake City, Utah: Deseret Book), 2003, 248.

Samuel Harrison Smith

By Glenn Rawson

WRITER, PRODUCER, AND HOST OF THE *JOSEPH SMITH PAPERS* AND *HISTORY OF THE SAINTS* TELEVISION SERIES

IT WAS ON AN EVENING in June 1830 in Mendon, New York, when Phineas, a circuit preacher, was on his way home. He stopped at the Tomlinson Inn in Mendon for dinner. While he was eating and talking with the family, a roughly dressed young stranger came up to Phineas holding out a book. "There is a book, sir, I wish you to read."

Phineas hesitated a moment and then said, "Pray, sir, what book have you?"

"The Book of Mormon," said the young man, "or, as it is called by some, the Golden Bible."

"Ah, then it purports to be a revelation," Phineas replied.

"Yes," said he. "It is a revelation from God."

Phineas took the book. It was new, and at the young man's direction, Phineas turned to the back of it and read the testimony of the witnesses. When he finished reading and looked up, the young man said, "If you will read this book with a prayerful heart and ask God to give you a witness you will know of the truth of this work."

"What is your name?" Phineas asked.

"My name is Samuel Harrison Smith."

"Ah," said Phineas, "you are one of the witnesses." "Yes," said he, "I know the book to be a revelation from God, translated by the gift and power of the Holy Ghost, and that my brother, Joseph Smith, Jun., is a Prophet, Seer and Revelator."

Skeptical at first, Phineas agreed to read the book, considering it his duty to prove all things and hold fast to that which was good. He read it twice over the next two weeks. Not only did he not find errors, he was converted. He then lent it to his father, who read it and declared it to be "the greatest work . . . he had ever seen." Phineas then gave it to his sister, who read it and declared it to be "a revelation." And so it went through the members of the family, each in turn believing the book to be a new revelation from God.

From that one book came the conversions and baptisms of Phineas, his father, his sister, and all his brothers, including, eventually, Brigham Young—the second President of the Church—and the family of Heber C. Kimball. That small group of believers soon numbered sixty and formed the Mendon Branch.

Samuel was called and set apart as a missionary just days after the Church was organized. With no training and armed with only a sure testimony and a knapsack full of books, he went out to fulfill his calling. Though he endured much and personally baptized no one, he changed the world forever. This is what the Lord meant when He said, "I call upon the weak things of the world, those who are unlearned and despised, to thresh the nations by the power of my spirit; and their arm shall be my arm" (D&C 35:13–14).

Sources

Lucy Mack Smith, *History of Joseph Smith by his Mother* (Salt Lake City, Utah: Deseret Book, 2009).

https://www.lds.org/new-era/2004/09/the-first-latter-day-missionary?lang=eng.

Saving the Book of Commandments

By Susan Easton Black
Emeritus professor of Church history and doctrine,
Brigham Young University

How precious is the word of the Lord to us?

In the fall of 1831, young Mary and her family moved to Independence, Missouri, where her Uncle, Algernon Sidney Gilbert, ran a dry goods and grocery store. The family was comfortable in their Missouri environs from 1831 to 1833—until tensions between Mormons and the old settlers erupted.

"One night a great many men got together and stoned our house, part of which was hewed logs and the other part or front was brick," Mary wrote. "After breaking all the windows they started tearing off the roof on the brick part, amidst awful oaths and yells that were terrible to hear."

More extreme violence followed. "I saw Bishop Partridge tarred and feathered, and also Brother Charles Allen," Mary penned. "My sister saw them cover them with tar, then empty a pillow of feathers over them. Oh what a sight, our hearts ached for them."

But it was not until the night that the "mob renewed their work again by tearing down the printing office" that the story of Mary and her sister Caroline risking their lives to save the word of God propelled them to center stage. Recalling that night, Mary penned, "My sister Caroline and I were in a corner of the fence, trembling, watching them." The sisters saw the mob bring out a pile of large sheets of paper, and heard one man say, "Here are the damned Mormon Commandments." At that point, Mary knew what they had to do. She "determined to have some of" the papers, even though it would put her life in grave danger. Her sister Caroline agreed to help her, but said, "They will kill us."

Relying on the mercies of the Lord to protect them, the sisters waited until the mob turned to pry "out the gable end of the [printing] building." They then "ran and got our arms full and were turning away when some of the mob saw us and called for us to stop," recalled Mary. "But we ran as fast as we could into a large cornfield, laid the papers on the ground and then we laid flat over them."

The corn was about five or six feet tall and "very thick." The mob "hunted quite a while for us, coming very near and making our hearts beat faster but finally left," Mary penned. After the sisters were satisfied that the men were gone, they came out of the cornfield and ran to safety.

The pages of scripture that were saved by the courageous actions of Mary and Caroline Rollins were later "bound in small books." Of the book given her, Mary wrote, "I prized it highly." Those few books would come to be one of Mormonism's rarest books. It was in November 1831 that a special "conference voted that they prize the revelations to be worth . . . the riches of the whole earth."

Source

"Autobiography of Mary E. Lightner," *Utah Genealogical and Historical Magazine* 17 (July 1926).

School of the Prophets

By Glenn Rawson

Writer, producer, and host of the *Joseph Smith Papers* and *History of the Saints* television series

Who could have known that out of such small beginnings would come forth such great things? It began in December 1832 when a revelation was received by the Prophet Joseph Smith that commanded, "I give unto you, who are the first laborers in this last kingdom, a commandment that you assemble yourselves together, and organize yourselves" (D&C 88:74).

Accordingly, on January 22, 1833, the School of the Prophets was organized with fourteen charter members. Among them were Joseph and Hyrum Smith, Orson Hyde, Orson Pratt, and Levi W. Hancock.

For the next three months, these men met in a small room on the second floor of the Newel K. Whitney Store. They had been instructed by revelation to "teach one another the doctrine of the kingdom" (D&C 88:77). Their curriculum was "of things both in heaven and in the earth; things which have been, things which are, things which must shortly come to pass, things which are at home, things which are abroad"

(D&C 88:79). In short, they were to learn everything about everything, and why? The Lord said, "That ye may be prepared in all things when I shall send you again to magnify the calling whereunto I have called you" (D&C 88:80).

The discipline expected of these men was extraordinary. They were to rise before dawn and come to school fasting and praying. They were to love one another and to cease from all laughter, light speech, pride, and all wicked doings. They were to retire to their beds early and arise early, and above all things they were to clothe themselves with charity.

After a full day of fasting and instruction, they partook of sacramental bread and wine, and the school closed for the day.

It was on February 27, 1833, that another revelation was received directed to those brethren—a revelation intended to purify them spiritually. Today we call it the Word of Wisdom.

On March 18, 1833, the Prophet Joseph boldly announced to the brethren that those sufficiently pure would see visions. On that day, sometime around noon, John Murdock described,

> The visions of my mind were opened, and the eyes of my understanding were enlightened and I saw the form of a man most lovely. The visage of his face was sound and fair as the sun. His hair a bright silver gray, curled in the most majestic form. His eyes a keen, penetrating blue, and the skin of his neck a most beautiful white. And he was covered from the neck to the feet with a loose garment, pure white, whiter than any garment I have ever before seen. His countenance was most penetrating, and yet most lovely. And while I was endeavoring to comprehend the whole personage from head to feet, it slipped from me and the vision was closed up. But it left on my mind the

> impression of love for months that I never felt before to that degree.

To have experienced such things, and to have spent three months learning at the feet of the Prophet Joseph—can you imagine? This was the first official Church school—the beginnings of the Church Educational System.

Source

Mark Lyman Staker, *Hearken O Ye People, The Historical Setting of Joseph Smith's Ohio Revelations* (Sandy, Utah: Greg Kofford Books, 2010).

http://josephsmithpapers.org/topic/school-of-the-prophets?p=1&highlight=school%20of%20the%20prophets.

The Ship Olympus

By Glenn Rawson

WRITER, PRODUCER, AND HOST OF THE *JOSEPH SMITH PAPERS* AND *HISTORY OF THE SAINTS* TELEVISION SERIES

ON MARCH 4, 1851, THE ship *Olympus* prepared to set sail from Liverpool, England, with 245 Latter-day Saint converts bound for America. Just before departure, Elder John Taylor prophesied that "the ship would encounter storms and furious gales, and be exposed to raging waves; that the Saints would have to contend with sickness, evil spirits and other troubles; but God would preserve them in the midst of all dangers, and lead them to a harbor of safety."

The ship set sail and almost immediately ran into fierce headwinds in the Irish Sea. The ship was tossed violently, and many passengers became seriously ill. One night a thirteen-year-old lad by the name of George McKenzie suddenly jumped from his bed, screaming the name of another passenger. It was quickly discerned the he was possessed by an evil spirit. After a chilling struggle, the evil spirits were cast out and the voyage continued.

It was calm Saturday afternoon on March 22, 1851, when Captain Wilson raised his hand to his brow and surveyed the horizon. Immediately, he ordered the sails shortened. The crew had not yet finished when a tiny cloud blossomed into a white squall. The storm struck the ship with such fury that the foremast was broken off and the main mast was sprung. The ship became unmanageable before the hurricane-force winds.

Throughout the evening, the captain and crew fought the storm. By 8 p.m., four feet of water filled the hold, and more was pouring in. By midnight the storm was not abated. Captain Wilson ordered his second mate, "You go to the captain of the Mormons and tell him from Captain Wilson that if the God of the Mormons can do anything to save the ship and the people, they had better be calling on Him to do so, for we are now sinking at the rate of a foot every hour; and if the storm continues we shall all be at the bottom of the ocean before daylight."

The man made his way below decks and, in the chaos, found President Howell in his bunk. Upon hearing the message, President Howell said in a surprisingly calm tone, "Very well. You may tell Captain Wilson that we are not going to the bottom of the ocean, for we embarked from Liverpool on a voyage for New Orleans, and we will arrive safely in that port. Our God will protect us."

As the message was returned, President Howell gathered the elders around and they began to pray in turn, each man vocally. The last man to pray was President Howell. In the midst of his prayer, the ship stopped pitching and rolling and instead trembled like a man with a cold. At the conclusion of the prayer, President Howell said, "You may all retire to your beds." All did except for one, who went above decks. To his astonishment, "the storm had miraculously ceased; the wind had gone down, and the waves were stilled immediately round about the ship, while in the distance the billows were still raging."

Captain Wilson, a coarse and profane man, would later declare "that he had done all that he could before calling on the 'Mormons,' and that no human power could have saved the ship."

In the end, the Saints did indeed arrive safely, and crew members of the Olympus were baptized and went on with the Saints.

That Lord who calmed the storm once can still do so, whether the raging storm is composed of nature's elements or is tucked within the darkness of the human heart.

Sources

Wilson G. Nowers, "Reminiscences," *Church Emigration Book*, vol. 2 (1850–54), 1–7.

http://mormonmigration.lib.byu.edu/Search/showDetails/db:MM_MII/t:account/id:1093.

Switching Stones

By Glenn Rawson

Storyteller on the *Sounds of Sunday* radio program

The scene would have looked ordinary enough: two men—one in his twenties and the other middle-aged—standing by the bank of a river, throwing and skipping stones across the stream. It was welcome exercise. But then, as the older man was searching for another stone, he saw one that looked very familiar. Without his companion's notice, he picked it up and slipped it into his pocket.

That older man was Martin Harris of Palmyra, New York. The other man at the Susquehanna River that day was Joseph Smith Jr. In those early summer days of 1828, Martin and Joseph worked in Joseph and Emma's small farm cabin on the banks of the Susquehanna River, translating the gold plates. They labored day after day in the translation process.

Most of the time, Joseph translated using the Urim and Thummim. Sometimes, for the sake of convenience, Joseph translated with the aid of the seer stone while Martin wrote down what Joseph said.

Martin explained the translating as follows: "By aid of the seer stone, sentences would appear and were read by the

Prophet, and written by Martin, and when finished he would say, 'Written,' and if correctly written, the sentence would disappear and another appear in its place. If not written correctly it would remain until corrected."

It was tiresome work. Their unused muscles would cry for relief. It was for that reason that they would walk the few steps to the river and throw stones for exercise. The stone that looked familiar to Martin that day on the shores of the river resembled Joseph's seer stone. A plan formed in Martin's mind—a test, if you will.

Martin took his rock and returned to the cabin. Somehow he switched it with the seer stone and then waited to see what would happen. If Joseph continued to translate as usual, then Martin would know that Joseph was a liar and a fraud. But if he didn't translate. . . .

Martin "said the Prophet remained silent, unusually and intently gazing in darkness, no traces of the usual sentences appearing. Much surprised, Joseph exclaimed, "Martin, what is the matter? All is as dark as Egypt."

Martin's countenance betrayed him, and he could not hide what he had done. When Joseph asked him why he had done such a thing, Martin replied, "To stop the mouths of fools."

Martin became convinced that the work was true. He would, notwithstanding great trial and affliction, bear witness to his last breath that Joseph Smith was a true prophet and that the Book of Mormon was of God.

The Prophet was once asked to tell how he translated the Book of Mormon. He responded by saying that "it was not intended to tell the world all the particulars of the coming forth of the book of Mormon." It was done by the gift and power of God, and it was indeed a miracle.

Sources

Deseret News, Dec. 28, 1881, 763.
http://josephsmithpapers.org/paperSummary/minute-book-2?p=15&highlight=tell%20the%20world%20all%20the%20particulars.

"Take This Book Home and Finish It"

By Matthew C. Godfrey
Managing historian, *Joseph Smith Papers*

Mary Elizabeth Rollins Lightner is perhaps best known in Church history as one of the girls who rescued pages of the newly printed Book of Commandments from the mob that attacked the Church's printing office in Independence, Missouri, in 1833. However, equally notable is the strong faith she exhibited in both Joseph Smith and the Book of Mormon at an early age.

In 1828, when she was only ten, Mary moved with her family to Kirtland, Ohio, where they lived with her uncle Sidney Gilbert. When Oliver Cowdery, Peter Whitmer Jr., Ziba Peterson, and Parley P. Pratt came to Kirtland to preach in the fall of 1830, Mary and her family were baptized. However, they apparently did not obtain a copy of the Book of Mormon at that time.

A couple of months later, Isaac Morley, a Kirtland Church member, received a copy of the book. Mary asked him if she could see it. When Morley handed the book to her, she "felt such a desire to read it" that she asked him if she could borrow it. Morley protested, stating that he had had little opportunity to read the book himself. However, Mary was so persistent that Morley finally let her take it on condition that she would return it to him the next morning.

Mary showed the book to her family, and they "all took turns reading it until very late in the night." "As soon as it was light enough to see," Mary resumed her reading. She even memorized 1 Nephi 1:1. When she returned the book to Morley, he said to her, "I guess you did not read much of it" and declared, "I don't believe you can tell me one word of it." Mary then recited 1 Nephi 1:1 from memory. "He gazed at me in surprise," Mary recalled, "and said, 'child, take this book home and finish it, I can wait.'"

Not many days later, Joseph Smith moved to Kirtland, staying with Newel K. Whitney, Sidney Gilbert's business partner. Whitney brought Joseph to the Gilberts' residence, where Joseph saw Isaac Morley's copy of the Book of Mormon and asked why the Gilberts had it. Sidney Gilbert told him that his niece Mary had borrowed it from Morley, whereupon Joseph asked to meet her. When Mary entered the room, she later remembered, the Prophet "looked at me so earnestly, I felt almost afraid." But he then approached her, "put his hands on my head and gave me a great blessing, the first I ever received, and made me a present of the book." This had a profound impact on Mary, who later remembered that, on this occasion, she "felt that he was a man of God, for he spoke with power, and as one having authority in very deed."

The young Mary would continue faithful in the Church, dying in 1913 in Utah. She would ever remember the power the Book of Mormon had on her at the young age of twelve and this first encounter with the Prophet.

President Ezra Taft Benson once said of the Book of Mormon, "There is a power in the book which will begin to flow into your lives the moment you begin a serious study of the book. You will find greater power to resist temptation. You will find the power to avoid deception. You will find the power to stay on the strait and narrow path" ("The Keystone of our Religion," Conference Report, October 1986).

Source

"Mary Elizabeth Rollins Lightner," *The Utah Genealogical and Historical Magazine* 17 (July 1926), 193–205.

The Vision

By Glenn Rawson

WRITER, PRODUCER, AND HOST OF THE *JOSEPH SMITH PAPERS* AND *HISTORY OF THE SAINTS* TELEVISION SERIES

IT IS AN ESTABLISHED TRUTH verified by thousands of witnesses that the Lord Jesus Christ rose from the tomb on Resurrection morning with a glorified and perfected body of flesh and bones. Moreover, when He rose, the Saints who had slept rose with Him. By these ancient testimonies we find our faith and hope. This is the story, last of all, of another witness of the Risen Christ.

On Thursday, February 16, 1832, Joseph Smith and his family were living in the home of John and Elsa Johnson in Hiram, Ohio. The day was cold, with temperatures standing near twenty degrees and nearly three feet of snow on the ground.

Upstairs in the southeast corner of the home, Joseph and his scribe, Sidney Rigdon, were translating the holy scriptures. They came to John 5:28–29, which quotes the Savior as saying, "Marvel not at this: for the hour is coming, in the which all that are in the graves shall hear his voice, And shall come forth; they who have done good unto the resurrection of life; and they who have done evil, unto the resurrection of damnation."

The Savior's words caused them to marvel. There was a current debate among the religionists of the day. Did the next world consist of just heaven or hell, or were there three different rewards, as some were teaching?

As they meditated on the subject, the Lord touched the eyes of their understandings and they were opened, and the glory of the Lord shone round about. And that began a series of visions lasting hours.

There may have been as many as twelve men in that room who saw the glory but not the vision. No one moved or spoke as Joseph and Sidney gazed up into heaven and described what they saw. One witness, Philo Dibble, said, "Joseph wore black clothes, but at this time seemed to be dressed in an element of glorious white, and his face shone as if it were transparent. . . . [He] sat firmly and calmly all the time in the midst of a magnificent glory, but Sidney sat limp and pale, apparently as limber as a rag." The two men saw many things, only a hundredth part of which they would ever share.

That vision would clarify as no other revelation did what glories and blessings would be bestowed upon men by the redemption and Resurrection of Jesus Christ. Hence, the significance of the first vision they saw that day:

> We beheld the glory of the Son on the right hand of the Father and received of his fulness . . . and now after the many testimonies which have been given of him, this is the testimony, last of all, which we give of him: that he lives! For we saw Him, even on the right hand of God; and we heard the voice bearing record that he is the Only Begotten of the Father—that by him, and through him, and of him, the worlds are and were created, and the inhabitants thereof are begotten sons and daughters unto God.

Christ lives—as verified by the vision given to Joseph and Sidney. Of that there should be no doubt!

Source

Mark Lyman Staker, *Hearken O Ye People, The Historical Setting of Joseph Smith's Ohio Revelations* (Sandy, Utah: Greg Kofford Books, 2010), 319–330.

Thomas Giles

By William G. Hartley

Retired professor of history, Brigham Young University

Mormon asked, "Have miracles ceased because Christ hath ascended into heaven?. . . Behold, I say unto you nay" (Moroni 7:27, 29). Miracles are just as much a part of the Lord's work now as they were in the days of the Lord Jesus.

Blind harpist Thomas Giles suffered a series of misfortunes while going west to Utah in Captain Edward Bunker's handcart company in 1856. As part of one of those experiences, Apostle Parley P. Pratt's blessing pulled him from near death and gave him a new life.

Thomas Giles was born and raised in Wales. One day while working in the coal mines, a large chunk of coal fell on him. His severe head injuries left him totally blind. Nevertheless, he continued to do his Church duties. Someone gave him a harp and, despite his blindness, he learned to play it well.

In 1856, Thomas and his wife, Margaret, decided to gather to Zion with their children—Joseph, aged nine; Hyrum, seven; and Maria, one. Reaching America and then Iowa City, the Giles family joined the Bunker handcart company. A friend, Alfred Reese, led the way and helped Thomas with the cart.

Near Fort Laramie, Margaret gave birth to a baby, Elizabeth, but the baby died; Margaret also died soon after. Because of Thomas's blindness, his two boys were sent back to travel in a wagon train not far behind.

Thomas continued with the handcart company but became seriously ill. Captain Bunker held up the company for two days, hoping Thomas would get well enough to keep going. Finally, Captain Bunker ordered the camp to move on but left two men behind to bury Thomas, who was expected to die within hours.

Meanwhile, the Bunker company had met up at Pacific Springs with Elder Parley P. Pratt and others who were eastbound for "the States." When Elder Pratt, who had known Brother Giles in Wales, learned about the Giles family losses and about Thomas Giles's condition, he hurried to see Thomas. He gave his friend a remarkable blessing. It promised that Giles should "instantly be healed and made well, that he should rejoin his company and arrive safely in the Salt Lake Valley; that he should there rear a family; and that because of his faithfulness he would be permitted to live as long as he wanted."

That blessing came to pass. Thomas recovered and rejoined the company. He reached the valley. To make a living, he put his musical talent to work playing the harp. He traveled through the settlements giving concerts. He drew large audiences to hear him play the harp and sing hymns and popular songs. He performed at dances, socials, and Church services. He became well known as "Zion's Blind Harpist." He remarried and lived to bless and name seven grandchildren. He died on November 2, 1895, after he had expressed a desire to go.

Sources

Priscilla M. Evans recollections in LeRoy R. and Ann W. Hafen, *Handcarts to Zion* (Glendale, California: Arthur H. Clark Company, 1960), 86–87.

Lyndia Carter, "A Blind Man and His Harp," *History Blazer*, March 1996, posted at http://historytogo.utah.gov/utah.

Three Sure Witnesses

By Glenn Rawson

STORYTELLER ON THE *SOUNDS OF SUNDAY* RADIO PROGRAM

IT IS AN ETERNAL PRINCIPLE that "in the mouth of two or three witnesses shall every word be established" (2 Corinthians 13:1). That principle has been repeatedly manifest, and the following story is no exception.

It was a pleasant summer day at about eleven o'clock in the morning in late June 1829 in the small community of Fayette, New York. Joseph Smith, Martin Harris, and Oliver Cowdery walked from the home of Peter Whitmer III out into a nearby field where their companion, David Whitmer, was plowing. Together they went into the woods about forty rods from the cabin. There they sat down on a log, talked a while, and then knelt and began to pray in faith—each in turn.

Joseph prayed first. At the conclusion of the first round, they then commenced again, but still there was no result. At that point, "Martin Harris proposed that he withdraw himself."

After Martin had left they knelt and prayed again. They had not been many minutes in prayer when they discovered "a light above [them] in the air of exceeding brightness. Simultaneous with the light came a strange entrancing influence which permeated

[them] so powerfully that [they] felt chained to the spot." It was accompanied with a "sensation of joy absolutely indescribable."

And, then, standing before them was an angel of the Lord. He held in his hands the gold plates from which the Book of Mormon had been translated. He turned the leaves of the record one by one so that they were visible to every man present. Addressing David Whitmer, he said, "David, blessed is the Lord, and he that keepeth his commandments."

"Immediately afterwards, [they] heard a voice from out of the bright light above [them] saying, 'these plates have been revealed by the power of God, and they have been translated by the power of God. The translation of them which you have seen is correct, and I command you to bear record of what you now see and hear.'"

There appeared about three feet away "a table, with many records on it—besides the plates of the Book of Mormon, also the sword of Laban, the Directors, and the interpreters." David would later declare that "human language could not describe [the] heavenly things and that which we saw."

At the close of the vision, Joseph went in search of Martin Harris. Upon finding him, Martin asked Joseph to join him in prayer. Before they had even finished, the same vision was opened again. Upon hearing and beholding, "Martin Harris cried out, apparently in ecstasy of joy, 'Tis enough; mine eyes have beheld,' and jumping up he shouted hosanna, blessing God, and otherwise rejoiced exceedingly."

The four men returned to the cabin and drafted a document that stands today in the front of the Book of Mormon. It begins, "Be it known unto all nations, kindreds, tongues, and people unto whom this work shall come. . . ." It is the testimony of the Three Witnesses.

In the Book of Mormon, three sure witnesses establish that the record testifies of Christ. They are Nephi, Jacob, and Isaiah. Today, three additional sure witnesses establish that the book is true and of God. And all the world will be judged according to that singular and powerful witness.

Sources

Richard Lloyd Anderson, *Investigating the Book of Mormon Witnesses* (Salt Lake City, Utah: Shadow Mountain, 2000).

http://scottwoodward.org/bookofmormon_witnesses_3witnesses_davidwhitmer_compositeinterview.html.

Timely Relief:
Alvah Tippets and the Lewis New York Branch

By Matthew C. Godfrey

Managing historian, *Joseph Smith Papers*

President Joseph F. Smith once said, "You must be obedient. Obedience is the first law of heaven. . . . When we are obedient we may be guided to the accomplishment of all that is required of us by our heavenly Father, for it is on this principle that the designs and purposes of God are accomplished" (Journal of Discourses, 16:248).

In 1834, Joseph Smith and the Church faced numerous financial problems. After persecution led to the expulsion of Church members from Jackson County, Missouri, in 1833, the Church was left without its Independence printing office and without the storehouse that Sidney Gilbert had been operating. But Church leaders still owed money for the goods in Gilbert's storehouse, and they also had to expend money to purchase a new printing press and equipment so that the Church could continue its publishing efforts.

In addition, Church leaders had gone into debt in the summer of 1833 to purchase land in Kirtland, Ohio, on which they were constructing the house of the Lord. Joseph Smith had also contributed a large amount of personal money and property to an expedition he led from Ohio to Missouri in the summer of 1834 (later known as Zion's Camp) to aid those Church members who had been driven from Jackson County. Facing a bleak financial situation, Joseph was greatly concerned in the fall of 1834.

As Joseph's worries mounted, a group of Saints in Lewis, Essex County, New York, decided that the time had come for them to act on direction provided by the Lord in a December 1833 revelation. According to Alvah Tippets, who may have been the leader of the branch in Lewis, around the first of September 1834, he and two others read the revelation, especially its instructions to Church branches to "gather together all their moneys" and send "wise men" to Missouri to purchase land in and around Jackson County, thereby helping to redeem Zion. They then knelt in prayer and asked "God to enable us to obey" these instructions. Upon arising, the three men directed the branch to meet together in fasting and prayer. At that meeting, the branch's members donated almost $850. Alvah's brother Joseph H. Tippets, his sister Caroline Tippets, and his cousin John H. Tippets were then sent to Kirtland to seek direction from the Prophet Joseph and the Kirtland high council as to whether they should proceed with land purchases in Missouri.

When the Tippets arrived in Kirtland, they met with the high council. Members of the council decided that the three Tippets should remain in Kirtland for the winter. Since they did not immediately need the money for land purchases, Caroline agreed to lend $150 of the money—which was apparently her own money—to Joseph Smith, and John H. Tippets agreed to loan another $280, providing Joseph with a total of $430.

To the Prophet Joseph, this money was truly heaven-sent. The day after the Tippets family made their loan, Joseph and Oliver Cowdery knelt in prayer and thanked God "for the relief" that the loan provided. How they used the money is not clear, but it was desperately needed at the time it came. Not many Church members know of the sacrifice, but their willingness to act on the Lord's direction was something that led Joseph to "rejoic[e] before the Lord."

Sources

John Harvey Tippets, *Autobiography*, ca. 1882, in Church History Library, Salt Lake City, Utah

Minutes, Nov. 28, 1834, http://josephsmithpapers.org/paperSummary/minutes-28-november-1834.

Joseph Smith, Journal, 29 November 1834, in Dean C. Jessee, Mark Ashurst-McGee, and Richard L. Jensen, eds., *Journals, Volume 1: 1832–1839*, vol. 1 of the Journals series of *The Joseph Smith Papers*, ed. Dean C. Jessee, Ronald K. Esplin, and Richard Lyman Bushman (Salt Lake City, Utah: Church Historian's Press, 2013).

"To Sell Our Lives"

By Steven M. Parkin
CIVIL ENGINEER

FRIENDLY NON-MORMONS SOMETIMES DEFENDED THE Latter-day Saints. One was Peter H. Burnett. On a cold day in the winter of 1839, Peter Burnett offered his life, if necessary, to protect the Prophet Joseph Smith and his associates.

The Prophet and Sidney Rigdon and others had been arrested the previous fall at Far West, Missouri, on extreme charges—including treason—and had finally been dispatched to the Liberty Jail to await a circuit court hearing in the spring. However, in January, Joseph Smith and Sidney Rigdon were taken from Liberty Jail to a courtroom in the nearby Clay County Courthouse for a preliminary hearing, thus securing a brief reprieve from the harsh dungeon-like conditions in the Liberty Jail.

Because of the cold weather, the court was held in a smaller room on the second floor of the courthouse, which was easier to keep warm. The smaller room accommodated fewer than a hundred citizens, who were largely incensed against the Mormons and disapproved of the hearings. Peter Burnett, a former Liberty newspaperman and young attorney assisting Alexander

Doniphan, felt that their clients were in imminent peril. Both attorneys and the judge were residents of Liberty and knew well the rugged nature of their neighbors, who declared they had come to "do injury." Indeed, Burnett feared his clients might be mobbed and the prisoners forcibly seized, and probably hung.

County Judge Joel Turnham, known as a just and fearless man who had the power to release the prisoners on their writ of habeas corpus, further enraged the crowd. That Turnham would presume to consider releasing the prisoners when a judge of higher rank had previously sent the prisoners to jail was galling to Joseph's enemies.

As the hearings opened, Burnett gave introductory remarks in defense of the prisoners, and the attorney general explained the charges against them. Sidney Rigdon, sickly and hardly able to sit up because of his weeks in Liberty Jail, spoke in his own defense and did remarkably well.

Doniphan then stood to give the closing remarks in defense of the Prophet Joseph. Burnett observed the "maddened crowd" which "foamed and gnashed their teeth," appearing wildly threatening in the close quarters of the room. As tension mounted, Burnett slipped his hand down onto his pistol—determined, as he said, "to spend his life, if necessary, to protect the life of the Prophet." He then whispered to his partner, "Doniphan! Let yourself out, my good fellow; and I will kill the first man that attacks you." Speaking of Doniphan, Peter Burnett said that his partner indeed "let himself out" in giving one of the "most eloquent speeches," he had ever heard.

All the while Burnett sat with his hand on his pistol, willing to do all he had promised himself to do. Burnett remembered that he and Doniphan were willing "to sell our lives" to protect their clients.

Waiting several days, Judge Turnham cautiously freed Rigdon, secretly releasing him at night to save him from the mob. Joseph and the others were returned to Liberty Jail, alive and unharmed, and held over for the circuit court in March.

Ironically, it was in Liberty Jail that the Prophet Joseph dictated the following words in a letter to Bishop Edward Partridge and to Joseph's wife Emma in March 1839: "We should waste and wear out our lives in bringing to light all the hidden things of darkness, wherein we know them; and they are truly manifest from heaven" (D&C 123:13).

Peter H. Burnett soon thereafter went west and served on the supreme courts of Oregon and California and as California's first territorial governor.

Sources

Peter H. Burnett, *Recollections and Opinions of an Old Pioneer* (New York: D. Appleton and Company, 1880), 54; in 1836, Burnett had been the publisher of The Far West, a frontier newspaper at Liberty, Clay County, Missouri.

F. Mark McKiernan, *The Voice of One Crying in the Wilderness: Sidney Rigdon* (Lawrence, Kansas: Coronado Press, 1971), 98.

Vienna Jacques

By Susan Easton Black
Emeritus professor of Church history and doctrine,
Brigham Young University

Until becoming dissatisfied with their religious tenets, Vienna Jacques attended the Methodist services at the Bromfield Street church in Boston. While investigating other Christian denominations, she learned of the Book of Mormon and sent for a copy. After glancing through the book, she laid it aside until a vision of the book convinced her to pick it up and read. As she read, her mind became "illuminated." Convinced of its truthfulness, forty-three-year-old Vienna traveled by canal boat and then by stage to Kirtland, Ohio, to meet the translator of the Book of Mormon, Joseph Smith.

Vienna remained in Ohio for about six weeks before returning to Boston, where she was instrumental in sharing the gospel with family members. Yet alone, she again journeyed to Kirtland. This time she brought with her $1,400, the sum total of her savings.

On March 8, 1833, the Prophet Joseph directed Vienna to give all of her monies to the Church. Without hesitation, she gave all of her savings to the Prophet. For her unselfish consecration, the Lord said, "My handmaid Vienna Jacques should receive money to bear her expenses, and go up unto the land of Zion." On consecrated funds Vienna journeyed to Zion—Independence, Missouri—and there received "an inheritance from the hand of the bishop." She settled on her land of inheritance and there recognized the mercies of the Lord in her behalf until mobs forced her to abandon the property.

Feeling discouraged, Vienna prayed, asking the Lord to "inspire thy servant Joseph to communicate by letter some word to thine unworthy handmaiden." Although residing more than nine hundred miles away in Kirtland and far from the scene of mobocracy that had become all too familiar to Vienna, the Prophet Joseph felt inspired to write on September 4, 1833, "I have often felt a whispering . . . 'Joseph, thou art indebted to thy God for the offering of thy sister, Vienna, which proved a savor of life as pertaining to thy pecuniary concerns. Therefore, she should not be forgotten of thee, for the Lord hath done this, and thou shouldst remember her in all thy prayers and also by letter, for she often times calleth on the Lord.'"

By letter to Vienna, the Prophet Joseph told of being forewarned of the struggles that she had encountered in Missouri: "I was aware when you left Kirtland that the Lord would chasten you, but I prayed fervently in the name of Jesus that you might live to receive your inheritance. . . . I am not at all astonished at what has happened to you."

As the years passed, Vienna was given another city lot—this one in the Salt Lake 12th Ward. On this lot, she lived out her days in "strict obedience to the commandments of God."

Sources

George Hamlin, "In Memoriam," *Woman's Exponent* 12, no. 19 (March 1, 1884): 152.

D&C 90:28–31.

Joseph Smith letter to Vienna Jaques, Sept. 4, 1833, *Joseph Smith Papers*, Church History Library.
History of the Church, 1:408.

"Where Is Your Faith?"

By Mary Jane Woodger
Professor of Church history and doctrine,
Brigham Young University

In December 1830 the Lord commanded His Church to move to Ohio (see D&C 37:3). Three groups immigrated: Newell Knight led sixty-seven Saints of the Colesville Branch, Martin Harris led fifty members of the Manchester Branch, and Lucy Mack Smith led eighty members of the Fayette Branch.

When Lucy Smith's group arrived in Buffalo in May 1831, the Colesville Branch was already stranded there due to the harbor being locked with ice. The Colesville Saints immediately informed Lucy's group not to tell anyone they were Mormons, or they would not find a boat or lodging. Lucy responded: "I shall tell people precisely who I am, and if you are ashamed of Christ, you must not expect to be prospered; and I shall wonder if we do not get to Kirtland before you!" The Colesville branch was engaged in murmuring, grumbling, flirting, and giggling, and those on the shore were witnessing the "scene of clamor and vanity . . . with great interest."

Forcing her way into the middle of the crowd, Lucy declared,

> Brethren and sisters, we call ourselves, saints, and profess to have come out from the world for the purpose of serving God at the expense of all earthly things; and will you, at the very onset, subject the cause of Christ to ridicule by your own unwise and improper conduct? You profess to put your trust in God, then how can you feel to murmur as you do? . . . Where is your faith? Where is your confidence in God? . . . All the saints here should raise their hearts in prayer to God that the way might be opened before us. How easy it would be for him to cause the ice to break away; so that in a moment's time we could be on our journey.

Lucy continued her exhortations until two in the morning, when the group petitioned God and went back on the boat. Then, "a noise was heard, like bursting thunder. The captain cried, 'Every man to his post.' The ice parted, leaving barely a passage for the boat, and so narrow, that as the boat passed through, the buckets of the waterwheel were torn off with a crash." The boat had barely passed through the opening when behind them the ice closed again, leaving most of the Colesville brethren unable to follow.

The boat was so loaded that onlookers were certain it would sink. In fact, one newspaper even published that the Mormon boat had sunk with all on board. When Lucy and the Saints miraculously arrived in Fairport, they were amused to read in the news of their own deaths.

"Without faith it is impossible to please Him" (Hebrews 11:6) This is that faith that pleases God and gets things done.

Sources

Fred E. Woods, "We Wanted to Come to Zion," *Ensign*, March 2005.
Lucy Mack Smith, *History, 1845*, 198, *Joseph Smith Papers, Histories*,

http://josephsmithpapers.org/paperSummary/lucy-mack-smith-history-1845?p=206.

Wilford Woodruff

By Susan Easton Black

Emeritus professor of Church history and doctrine,
Brigham Young University

"I have been inspired and moved upon to keep a journal and write the affairs of this Church as far as I can," said Wilford Woodruff. For sixty-three years he kept a written record of the history of the Church. Wilford said, "I seldom ever heard Brother Joseph or the Twelve preach or teach any principle but what I felt as uneasy as a fish out of water until I had written it. Then I felt right. I could write a sermon of Joseph's a week after it was delivered almost word for word, and after it was written, it was taken from me, or from my mind. This was a gift from God unto me."

Yet in so doing, Wilford faced many afflictions and came to know that "the devil knew if I got into the Church of Jesus Christ of Latter-day Saints, I would write the history of that Church and leave on record the works and teachings of the prophets, of the apostles and elders."

Of his life experiences, Wilford wrote, "I have broken both legs—one in two places—both arms, my breast bone and three ribs, and had both ankles dislocated. I have been drowned, frozen, scalded and bit by a mad dog—have been in two water wheels under full head of water—have passed through several severe fits of sickness, and encountered poison in its worst forms—have landed in a pile of railroad ruins—have barely been missed by the passing bullets, and have passed through a score of other hair-breath escapes."

Wilford recognized the mercy of the Lord in preserving his life:

> It has appeared miraculous to me, that with all the injuries and broken bones which I have had, I have not a lame limb, but have been enabled to endure the hardest labor, exposures and journeys—have often walked forty, fifty, and one occasion, sixty miles in a day. The protection and mercy of God has been over me, and my life thus far has been preserved; for which blessings I feel to render the gratitude of my heart to my Heavenly Father, praying that the remainder of my days may be spent in His service and in the building up of His kingdom.

"And in nothing doth man offend God, or against none is his wrath kindled, save those who confess not his hand and obey not his commandments" (D&C 59:21).

Sources

Journal of Wilford Woodruff, March 17, 1857.

Matthew Cowley, *Wilford Woodruff, Fourth President of the Church of Jesus Christ of Latter-day Saints: History of His Life and Labors as Recorded in His Daily Journals* (Salt Lake City, Utah: Bookcraft, 1964), 477.

"History of Wilford Woodruff (From His Own Pen): Chapter of Accidents," *Millennial Star*, June 24, 1865, 392.

Willard Gilbert Smith

By Glenn Rawson

Storyteller on the *Sounds of Sunday* radio program

The angry mob rode into the small Latter-day Saint settlement of Hawn's Mill, Missouri, howling like demons and shooting at everything that moved. The call for quarter was answered with more bullets. Women and children screamed and ran for the woods while most of the men and boys ran into the blacksmith shop for defense.

Willard Smith ran with his father and brothers, but when he tried to enter the shop, his arms inexplicably flew up and prevented him—three times! Desperate for cover, he buried himself in a nearby woodpile, but the mob shot into the wood, splintering it all around him.

Willard then ran for a nearby cabin. There he found Father McBride terribly wounded. The old man asked for a drink of water. Willard ran to the millpond and, notwithstanding bullets raining like hail around him, he returned to the old man with the water.

He ran on to another cabin nearby. As he entered, bullets smashed into the wood behind him. He heard whimpering and soft voices. Lifting the valance on the bed, he discovered six little girls beneath, huddled in fear. Willard knew the mob would be there in moments. "Come," he cried. "We must get out of here or we will all be killed."

Willard led the girls from the cabin and across the mill pond, bullets striking all around them. From there, the girls vanished into the woods and safety.

When the mob had finished their murder and looting, they rode off howling. Willard was the first to come out of hiding and survey the holocaust—the first to enter the blacksmith shop and discover his father and younger brother dead. He pulled Alma, his other brother, grievously wounded, out of the pile of bodies and carried him out to his mother.

As darkness fell, cattle bellowed, dogs howled, and terror gripped the survivors. Willard spoke of his personal terror as his mother sent him into the darkness in search of roots to minister to his wounded brother.

"It required all the courage I could summon," he said, "to take the shovel, and with the aid of a dim torch, follow the stream and secure the roots from which Mother made a soothing poultice."

The next day, Willard would face a task that even the strongest men in the camp could not bear. With his mother, he dropped the body of his slain brother into a dry well to keep him from the depredations of the mob.

Willard would ever after speak admiringly of his mother, Amanda Barnes Smith. Her faith and example inspired courage in him. Five weeks after that attack, Willard would go with his mother to face the mob and retrieve their stolen horse.

And all of this remarkable courage from a boy only eleven years old!

Willard Smith would go on to be a temple-builder, member of the Mormon Battalion, missionary, husband, father, bishop, and stake president. He is buried in Morgan, Utah.

"And if you keep my commandments and endure to the end you shall have eternal life, which gift is the greatest of all the gifts of God" (D&C 14:7).

Sources

Tragedy and Truth: What Really Happened at Hawn's Mill (American Fork, Utah: Covenant Communications, Inc., 2014).

http://mormonhistoricsites.org/wp-content/uploads/2013/04/11-MHS_2007_Willard-GIlbert-Smith-Hauns-Mill-Massacre.pdf.

"You Shall Be Made Whole"

By Mary Jane Woodger
Professor of Church history and doctrine,
Brigham Young University

During the antipolygamy persecution, some Church leaders required bodyguards. One Latter-day Saint who served in this capacity was Joseph W. McMurrin. One day he was guarding the servants of the Lord while they were holding a meeting in the Social Hall.

During the meeting, a United States marshal came to the back door and tried to enter the hall. McMurrin, being true to his trust to guard the brethren, restrained the deputy from going through the door. The intruder finally got his hand loose, took his pistol, and, pressing it against McMurrin's body, fired two bullets clear through his vitals. Those bullets lodged just under the skin in his back.

McMurrin was immediately taken to Dr. Joseph Benedict, who told McMurrin that no man could survive such an injury. He added, "If you wish to make a dying statement you should do so immediately."

Elders Heber J. Grant and John Henry Smith immediately came to the McMurrin home and saw where the flesh was burned away around two terrible gaping wounds. In the process of a priesthood blessing, John Henry Smith promised, "By the authority of the Priesthood of the living God which we hold, and in the name of the Lord, Jesus Christ, we say that you shall be made absolutely whole, and that there shall be no physical weakness left upon your body because of these terrible wounds that you have received while guarding the servants of the living God."

Later, on November 21, 1931, President Grant reported that "Joseph W. McMurrin is alive and well, and has never had any physical weakness because of those terrible wounds."

"And the elders of the Church, two or more, shall be called, and shall pray for and lay their hands upon them in my name, and if they die they shall die unto me, and if they shall live unto me" (D&C 42:44).

Source

Heber J. Grant, *Gospel Standards: Selections From The Sermons and Writings of Heber J. Grant, Seventh President of The Church Of Jesus Christ of Latter-Day Saints* (Salt Lake City, Utah: Bookcraft, 1998), 310.